Inspired Imperfection

Inspired Imperfection

How the Bible's Problems Enhance Its Divine Authority

GREGORY A. BOYD

FORTRESS PRESS
MINNEAPOLIS

INSPIRED IMPERFECTION
How the Bible's Problems Enhance Its Divine Authority

Cover image: Beboy/Adobe Stock
Cover design: Paul Soupiset

Print ISBN: 978-1-5064-5562-4
eBook ISBN: 978-1-5064-5563-1

To the remarkable pastors and staff of
Woodland Hills Church.
Thank you for your willingness to think,
for your courage to act,
and for your refusal to ever let anything
compromise our call
to do everything in love.

Contents

Acknowledgments ix

Introduction xi

Part I. Wrestling with "Problems"

1. An Inconvenient Truth 3
2. A Better Foundation 15
3. Between Scylla and Charybdis 28
4. Taking Another Look 37
5. Searching for a Safe Zone 44
6. Game Changer 50
7. Foundational Insights 63
8. Critiquing Barth 72

Part II. Cruciform Inspiration

9. Epicenter 85
10. The Foolish and Weak Bible 97

11. Cruciform Breathing 106
12. Cruciform Power 116
13. Cruciform Accommodation 125
14. Cruciform Beauty 140
15. Back to the Conundrum 152

Postscript: Beautiful Scars 167
Glossary 173
Author Index 179
Topic Index 182

Acknowledgments

As has held true of everything I have ever written, I am keenly aware of how much *Inspired Imperfection* is indebted to others. For starters, I am blessed beyond measure to pastor an unusual, passionate, Christ-centered, Bible-based, evangelical-Anabaptist church—Woodland Hills Church in Maplewood, Minnesota—that supports their senior pastor writing a potentially controversial book like this! Thank you, Woodland Hills, for always being willing to join in my exploration of new ways of looking at old problems. I am honored to have been your pastor over the last twenty-seven exciting years.

I want to offer a more particular word of gratitude to the remarkable ten students who belonged to the first-year class of the School of Missional Apprenticeship (SOMA) that is now part of Woodland Hills. Thank you for the engaging conversations we had around biblical authority and the cross, as well as around so many other matters. I hope our time together will prove as profitable for the kingdom in your life as it has been for mine.

I must also express my profound appreciation for the remarkable pastors and staff of Woodland Hills Church, to whom this book is dedicated. I doubt there are many pastoral teams on the planet that spend as much time and energy discussing contested theological issues as we do. I love that we are odd like this, and I, for one, am the better for it.

A special word of appreciation must be given to Janice Rohling, the executive pastor at Woodland Hills for the last twenty-two years. God has used this extraordinary (and extraordinarily *strange*) woman to not only create the unique other-oriented staff culture we have at Woodland Hills but also prophetically guide our church at crucial junctures in our history. Janice, the longer I have the opportunity to minister alongside of you, the more appreciative I've become of the precious gift that you are to Woodland Hills Church and to the body of Christ as a whole.

As is true of almost everything I've ever written, this book is heavily indebted to my beloved covenant bro, Paul Eddy. I love the way our polar-opposite personalities and gift mixes complement each other. Among other things, were it not for the editorial work of my much-more-cautious covenant brother, I am quite sure my tendency to state things in bold but insufficiently nuanced ways would have made this work less compelling, especially to some conservative readers. Thank you, Paul, for always watching my back!

Finally, I am not exaggerating when I profess that nothing in my life would work without my truly remarkable wife of forty years, Shelley (a.k.a. Beso). Beso is super smart in all the ways I'm exceptionally stupid, including in just about everything practical. I am acutely aware of the fact that I could not begin to do what I do, including writing books, were it not for Beso's willingness to serve as a buffer of sorts between me and the practical world. Beso, the selfless and always-behind-the-scenes way in which you pour yourself out for me, for our children, and for our grandchildren, as well as for our friends, neighbors, and strangers, makes you a kingdom rock star in my book!

Words cannot express how blessed I feel to have such a kingdom rock star as my life-long partner and friend!

Introduction

I became a Christian in 1974, several weeks after my seventeenth birthday. I surrendered my life to Jesus in a small Pentecostal revival service where I had a powerful, even life-transforming, encounter with God.

This particular Pentecostal church placed a lot of importance on people experiencing God in dramatic, emotionally charged ways. It was, for them, the main proof that their particular doctrines—some of which, I would later learn, were quite unorthodox—were true.[1] Consequently, I ended up having a number of emotionally charged experiences with God in the year following my conversion, which is why I initially embraced everything this church taught, including the teaching that the Bible is "the divinely inspired, completely inerrant, word of God," as my pastor regularly preached.

I was also taught that true Christians—as opposed to those liberal Christians—accept that everything in the Bible is *literally* true. "If the earth wasn't created in six literal days," I remember my pastor preaching, "then the whole Bible may as well be a book of lies."

I had been an atheist for four years leading up to my conversion, and I had increasingly struggled with the apparent meaninglessness of life. Now, however, I felt like my life had an eternal purpose, and *I loved it.* I wasn't certain of anything

1. For my critical assessment of the teachings of the Oneness Pentecostal movement, which this church was a part of, see G. Boyd, *Oneness Pentecostals and the Trinity* (Grand Rapids: Baker, 1992).

prior to my conversion but afterwards, my dramatic experiences of God made me feel certain I had "found the truth," as we used to say in my Pentecostal Church. I enjoyed that blissful certainty and sense of purpose throughout my senior year in high school.

Then I attended the University of Minnesota (U of M), and that bliss went straight out the window.

* * *

As has happened to countless other young Christians who have been taught that the Bible must be inerrant if it is to be considered divinely inspired, my year-old-faith came crashing down once I discovered that the Bible is plagued with all sorts of errors. Two classes did the trick.

The first was a class entitled Introduction to Evolutionary Biology. I intentionally chose this class to pick a fight. I had prepared myself by reading three books that claimed to refute evolution and to prove Young Earth Creationism.[2] Because I hadn't been much of a reader up to this point in my life, I naively assumed that reading *three whole books* on a topic qualified me as something of an expert. I felt entirely too confident. My plan for this class was to use my "expert" knowledge of "the truth" to expose the lie of evolution and to thereby save the faith of fellow Christians in this class. Perhaps, I fantasized, I might even convert some nonbelievers. My fantasy failed spectacularly.

Today, I am astonished, and frankly a bit embarrassed, by the naïve arrogance of my ridiculous eighteen-year-old self. Every day for the first several weeks of this course, I would come to class with a stack of three-by-five cards, each of which contained a summary of an anti-evolution or a pro-Creationism argument that I had transcribed from one of the three books I'd read. Whenever our professor would make a point that I had an argument against, I would raise my hand, find the relevant three-by-five card, and voice my objection. Each and every

2. In case you're wondering, the three books were J. Whitcomb, H. Morris, *The Genesis Flood: The Biblical Record and Its Scientific Implications* (Philipsburg, NJ: P & R Publishing, 1961); H. Morris, *Scientific Creationism* (Green Forest. AR: Master Books, 1974); and D. Gish, *Evolution: The Fossils Say No* (USA: Institute for Creation Research, 1973).

time, my professor would calmly and effortlessly expose the weakness or factual incorrectness of my objection, and then move on.

I quickly surmised that I wasn't the first fundamentalist Christian this professor had tangoed with. By the third or fourth class, some students began to complain about my persistent questioning. It was an annoying distraction, they claimed, and, looking back at it, they were completely right. To my great surprise, however, this professor actually *defended* me! "It's always good to critically reexamine our foundational assumptions in science," he would say with a gentle smile.

The respectful way this professor interacted with me, despite my obnoxious questioning, was itself a challenge to my faith. From my Pentecostal church, I had inherited the baseless assumption that any professor who taught evolution must be a godless, mean, and anti-Christian person. This gracious professor was blowing apart this absurd fundamentalist stereotype, and it frankly irritated me. I wanted so badly *not* to like him. Looking back on it, I think it was the kindness of this professor that produced the first crack in my religious-experience-based certainty. Apparently not *everything* my church believed was true.

It took me a little less than four weeks to burn through all my flash cards and, much to the delight of my fellow students, to finally shut up. By the time the course ended, nine weeks later, I saw no way of denying that the earth was several billion years old or that humans were the product of a 560-million-year evolutionary process. As painful as it was for me to admit, the evidence was simply irrefutable. Unfortunately for me, I still believed what my pastor had taught me: "If the earth wasn't created in six literal days, then the whole Bible may as well be a book of lies." Convinced that the earth wasn't created in six literal days, I felt I had no choice but to reject the book of lies.

My biology class might have sufficed to topple my faith by itself, but it didn't need to try. It received strong assistance from another freshmen course I attended called, "The Bible as Literature." Unlike my biology class, it never occurred to me that this class would challenge my faith. In fact, since I had already read the entire Bible and heard a year's worth of sermons on it, I assumed this would probably be the easiest three credits I'd ever earn. They ended up being the hardest.

As I will share in the first chapter, this course convinced me that the Bible contained a multitude of errors, contradictions, and historical inaccuracies, as well as morally offensive material. And as was the case when I reluctantly accepted the theory of evolution, I assumed this meant I had to abandon my faith and return to my pre-Christian atheism and the meaninglessness of life that came with it. It devasted me. I sunk into the deepest and longest depression of my life.

I'll pick up that story in the following chapter.

* * *

Countless numbers of young (and occasionally older) evangelical Christians have gone through something similar to what I went through. First, they base their faith on a supposedly inerrant Bible. They then take a course or read a book or talk to an informed person who demonstrates to them that the Bible contains errors. Consequently, they lose their faith. And while I obviously found my way back to the faith and managed to eventually make sense of these problems in the Bible—this is, after all, what this book is all about—many who lose their faith over these problems do not. One of the reasons I decided to write this book is because I would love to see this unnecessary tragedy stop repeating itself.

Unlike many who consider themselves evangelicals, broadly defined, I don't believe the way to do this is by trying to explain away or downplay the Bible's errors or by continually redefining what an "error" is. Rather, the way to stop this, I believe, is to subvert the assumption that the divine inspiration of the Bible is incompatible with it containing normal human errors.

Not to get too far ahead of myself, but consider this: If God perfectly revealed Godself in history through a man who bore the sin of the entire human race, why should we for a moment think it a problem for God to reveal Godself through a book that reflects the fallenness and fallibility of its human authors? The claim that I'll be defending in this book is that, if we anchor our conception of divine inspiration in the cross, as I will argue we should, we are able to see how the Bible's so-called "problems" are not genuine problems that need to be solved; they actually *contribute to* the inspired authority and central message of Scripture.

* * *

A second concern that led to the writing of this book has to do with what I see happening among *progressive evangelicals*.*[3] While progressive evangelicals generally affirm that the Bible is, in some sense, divinely inspired, they also tend to accept the legitimacy of the *historical-critical approach to Scripture*.* Which means, among other things, that they generally accept that the Bible contains errors, contradictions, inaccuracies, and morally offensive material.

Some progressive evangelical authors are content to simply chalk such things up to the fact that, while the Bible is in some sense inspired, it also was written by fallible humans. So too, some progressive evangelicals are content to explain away morally offensive depictions of God—the depiction of Yahweh commanding the extermination of the Canaanites, for example—by arguing that the stories that contain such depictions are not historically accurate and that God allows people to tell God's story from their own culturally conditioned perspective.[4]

I deeply appreciate the fact that these colleagues have been willing to honestly grapple with Scripture's violent depictions of God as well as with other challenging aspects of Scripture. And for the most part, I completely agree with them. For example,

3. Since I'm writing this book for a general audience, I have a glossary of words and phrases at the end of this book that a general audience might not be familiar with. The first use of these words or phrases will be italicized and marked with an asterisk (*).

4. See, for example, E. Seibert, *Disturbing Divine Behavior: Troubling Old Testament Images of God* (Minneapolis, MN: Fortress, 2009); P. Enns, *The Bible Tells Me So . . . Why Defending Scripture Has Made Us Unable to Read It* (New York: HarperOne, 2014); D. Flood, *Disarming Scripture: Cherry-Picking Liberals, Violence-Loving Conservatives, and Why We All Need to Learn to Read the Bible Like Jesus Did* (San Francisco: Metanoia Books, 2014).

while I am generally impressed with the archeological support for many portions of Scripture, I do not have a problem accepting that some portions of Scripture, including portions containing violent depictions of God, may not be solidly anchored in history. Nor do I dispute that, generally speaking, God lets God's people tell God's story from their own culturally conditioned perspective. Indeed, as will become clear as this book unfolds, I think this is a profoundly important point all Bible readers need to remember! Where I part ways with my colleagues, however, is when they conclude that these sorts of explanations suffice to render Scripture's violent depictions of God nonproblematic.

The traditional teaching of the church is that *all* Scripture is "God-breathed."[5] This is what has become commonly known as the "plenary (full) inspiration of *Scripture**." If we accept this teaching, as I do, these sorts of explanations cannot be considered adequate. The plenary inspiration of Scripture has always been understood to require adherents to consider every passage of Scripture to be God-breathed and to therefore contribute something to the revelatory content of Scripture. Indeed, Jesus himself taught, and the church has always confessed, that all Scripture is God-breathed for the ultimate purpose of pointing people to Jesus Christ.[6] We may therefore conclude that a passage containing a violent depiction of God is historically inaccurate and that God allowed God's people to tell God's story from their own perspective, but this doesn't remove our need to discern how these inspired violent depictions of God point to Jesus.

Unless, of course, we simply abandon the plenary inspiration of Scripture, which is precisely what I fear some progressive evangelicals are doing. I consider this a grave mistake. Among other things, denying Scripture's plenary inspiration is

5. In 2 Tim 3:16, Paul (or a disciple of Paul) uses the word *theopnuestos*, which literally means "God-breathed" (from *theos* [God] and *pneustos* [breath]). For a variety of reasons I need not go into here, I prefer this translation over the more common translation of this word as "divinely inspired." I prefer this despite the fact that talk about God "breathing" admittedly sounds a bit peculiar. Nevertheless, I will continue to use "divinely inspired," or simply "inspired," whenever "God-breathed" feels too awkward or is getting too repetitious.

6. John 5:39–45; Luke 24:24–27, 44–47.

inconsistent not only with the church tradition, but, as I will later argue, with the teachings of Jesus and some New Testament (NT) authors. Not only this, but history demonstrates that when groups relinquish the church's traditional view of Scripture, they tend eventually to float outside the parameters of *historic orthodox Christianity*.* I consider the recent Emergent Church phenomenon to be a case in point.[7]

Finally, a second century theologian named Origen taught that, when we come upon material in the Bible that seems "unworthy of God," we must try not to get angered or offended by it, and we certainly must never reject it, for it is all divinely inspired. Instead, Origen taught, we must humble ourselves, call on the Spirit to enlighten us, and keep searching for a deeper meaning that *is* "worthy of God."[8]

Like a precious treasure buried beneath the ground, Origen held that many of Scriptures deepest revelatory insights can only be unearthed by patiently digging for them. Indeed, Origen believed God-breathed Scripture contained problems precisely so disciples would mature by patiently digging deeper while learning how to humbly lean on the Spirit's guidance.

My concern is that when people lose confidence in the plenary inspiration of Scripture and thus feel free to reject biblical material because it's problematic, they won't feel the need to keep digging when they confront the Old Testament's (OT) violent depictions of God, or any of the Bible's other problematic material. They will thereby forfeit all the benefits this digging can produce, including the possibility of discovering hidden treasures. And what makes this point particularly important is that Origen believed, and I fully agree, that these hidden treasures are all reflections of Jesus Christ.

My hope is that this book helps some progressive evangelicals recover their belief in the plenary inspiration of Scripture and consider the deeper cross-centered meaning behind the Bible's

7. While I think he is at times a bit too harsh, see D. A. Carsen, *Becoming Conversant with the Emerging Church* (Grand Rapids: Zondervan, 2005).

8. For a comprehensive exposition, see G. Boyd, *The Crucifixion of the Warrior God: How the Cross Makes Sense of the Old Testament's Violent Portraits of God*, 2 vols. (Minneapolis: Fortress, 2017), 1:417–61.

problems that I will be proposing, a meaning that reveals how these so-called problems actually bear witness to the cross.

Yet, as concerned as I am about Christian students losing their faith and progressive evangelicals floating outside the stream of historic-Christian-orthodoxy, I would have written this book even if I hadn't had these concerns, which brings me to the third reason I wrote this book.

* * *

Jürgen Moltmann once claimed that "the secret that unlocks all the mystery of Christian doctrine is found in the cross."[9] Over the last fifteen years, and for reasons to be discussed in this book, I have become convinced that Moltmann is absolutely right! I believe that everything we believe about God and God's relationship to us must be anchored in the crucified Christ.[10]

In this book, I will be applying Moltmann's insight to our understanding of biblical inspiration. The question I will be addressing is this: What does the definitive revelation of God on the cross teach us about the manner in which God breathed Scripture? More specifically, I want to explore how anchoring our conception of inspiration in the cross fundamentally alters how we understand the Bible's errors, contradictions, inaccuracies, and morally offensive material. And, as I've already alluded, my thesis is that, when understood in light of the cross, these problems become *assets* to what God inspired Scripture to accomplish: leading people to Jesus Christ.

I will label this cross-based understanding of inspiration the

9. J. Moltmann, *The Crucified God: The Cross of Christ as the Foundation and Criticism of Christian Theology*, trans. R. A. Wilson and J. Bowden (Minneapolis, MN: 1993), 114.

10. Whenever I refer to "the crucified Christ" or "the cross" throughout this book, I am not referring to Jesus's crucifixion *in contrast to* his life, teaching and ministry, but as the summation and culminating expression of his life, teaching and ministry. I contend that the love of God revealed on the cross is the through line that weaves together everything Jesus was about from his incarnation to his ascension. On the thematic unity of Jesus's ministry, from the incarnation to the ascension, see T. F. Torrance, "The Continuous Union in the Life of Jesus," in his *Incarnation: The Person and Life of Christ*, ed. R. T. Walker (Downers Grove, IL: IVP Academic, 2008), 105–60. For a discussion and scholarly sources supporting this perspective, See Boyd, *Crucifixion of the Warrior God*, 1:161–71.

*Cruciform Model of Inspiration.** I certainly hope this model helps Christian students retain their faith and helps progressive evangelicals recover their confidence in the plenary inspiration of Scripture. But even apart from these concerns, I consider the goal of arriving at a cross-centered understanding of how God breathes, and thus a cross-centered understanding of how and why God breathes all the problems found in Scripture, to be extremely important in and of itself.

* * *

Before discussing the outline of this book, there are several preliminary matters that need to be briefly discussed. The first concerns the way I will speak about God in this book. Because women and men are created equally in the image of God, it should go without saying that God is no more masculine than feminine, or, if you prefer, just as feminine as masculine. The fact that the Bible speaks of God in predominantly (though not exclusively) masculine terms must therefore be understood to reflect God's accommodation of the patriarchalism of the cultures in which the Bible was written.

Over the last several years I have become increasingly convinced that, while God apparently needed to accommodate the patriarchalism of the ancient world, we need not, and should not, accommodate it any longer. As feminist theologians have been arguing for years, when groups rely exclusively on masculine pronouns and metaphors to talk about God, they tend to forget that they're speaking metaphorically. As a result, they tend to assume, however subconsciously, that God is *actually* more masculine than feminine.

By contrast, when masculine metaphors and pronouns are accompanied with feminine or gender-neutral metaphors, it serves to remind us that we are speaking metaphorically and that God actually transcends our gender distinctions.

Furthermore, when people assume, however subconsciously, that God is more masculine than feminine, they are also assuming that women are *less* in the image of God then men. And when an entire community embraces this subconscious prejudice, it is typically reflected in the subordinate roles women are given within the church. This is tragic not only because it prevents women from exercising their God-given gifts of leadership, but also because it hampers the ministry of the church by squandering these much-needed gifts.

Finally, when people rely exclusively on masculine language when talking about, or to, God, they are generally much less open to envisioning and experiencing the feminine dimension of God's perfection. They may know God as Father, but rarely, if ever, will they know God as Mother. And this, I believe, is most unfortunate. I have to confess that my own walk with God would be greatly diminished if I didn't relate to God as both Father and Mother. Indeed, for reasons I can't go into at present, experiencing the motherly love of God has been the single most healing aspect of my relationship with God.[11] And this makes me wonder how many other Christians might experience greater healing, freedom and wholeness if they were able to imagine and experience the feminine dimension of God's loving character.

What makes this challenging is that, if an author or speaker begins to refer to God as "she" or as "Mother" to an audience that has always relied exclusively on masculine pronouns and metaphors in their God-talk, this linguistic change immediately becomes the focus of this speaker's audience instead of whatever it was that she was trying to communicate. And since I am hoping that this book will be read by evangelicals, who tend to use exclusively masculine language for God, this is a concern I must take seriously.

At the same time, things won't ever change if authors and speakers aren't willing to push back on socio-linguistic norms. So, I've tried to strike a balance of sorts in this book. As you may have already noticed, I will use "God" and "Godself" (rather than "he" and "himself") when referring to God, the first Person of the Trinity, or when referring to God as Trinity. For obvious reasons, I will use "he" and "himself" when referring to Jesus. And, since "Spirit" (*pneuma*) is feminine in Greek, and since there is some precedent for this in the church tradition, I will use

11. For the background on my convictions regarding the motherhood of God, see my November 11, 2018 sermon entitled, "Where's Mommy?," whchurch.org/sermon/wheres-mommy.

"she" and "herself" whenever I refer to the Holy Spirit. I'm sorry if you find this a little distracting, but I encourage you to press on. You will (I hope) eventually get used to it.

* * *

Another preliminary word I need to make concerns the fact that, while it is traditional to refer to the Bible as "the word of God," I think it is generally more helpful to refer to it as "the story of God." For one thing, the Bible *is* a story, not a straightforward "word." Moreover, "word of God" easily gives the impression that the Bible came straight out of God's mouth; whereas, "the story of God" allows for multiple authors writing from multiple perspectives, which is how God's story is actually told in Scripture.

The final and most important thing I'd like to say about this point is that the Bible teaches that Jesus is the one and only Word of God. If Scripture is also to be referred to as "the word of God," it is only in the derivative sense that it is inspired for the ultimate purpose of pointing people to Jesus, who is the Word of God. Yet, this dual usage has often blurred the distinction between Jesus and the Bible, and the result has been *bibliolatry*.* To prevent this, I think it helpful to distinguish between Jesus, who is the Word of God, and Scripture, which is the divinely inspired and multiauthored story of God that bears witness to the Word.

* * *

The last preliminary word I'd like to offer concerns the restricted focus of this book. After helping readers appreciate the issues I'm wrestling with by sharing the story of my own struggles with the Bible in part 1, my only goal in part 2 is to outline and defend the Cruciform Model of Inspiration and to demonstrate how it transforms the Bible's problems into assets. Which means, among other things, that the goal of this book is *not* to introduce readers to general principles of sound exegesis and hermeneutics, let alone to weigh in on the multitude of issues that surround this field. There are plenty of books on the market that already do this.[12]

Moreover, while I will touch on various models of inspiration in the course of telling my story, it lies outside the scope of this book to engage in anything like a comprehensive and detailed exploration of all the various models of inspiration that have been proposed in church history or that are available today. There are plenty of books on the market that already do this as well.[13] This book is singularly focused on one issue (though it's a massive one), and it offers one cross-centered resolution to this issue. Expect anything more from this book, and I'm afraid you'll be disappointed.

* * *

Here is the broad road map for what is to follow.

This book is broken down into two parts. In part 1, I introduce readers to the problems in the Bible and to the various ways evangelical authors have wrestled with them by telling my own story of struggling with these problems. Chapters 1–5 cover my wrestling with Scripture while a student at the U of M and at Yale Divinity School (YDS). Chapters 6–8 then discuss how my encounter with the writings of Karl Barth, while attending Princeton Theological Seminary (PTS), brought about a complete paradigm shift in my thinking on biblical inspiration. This sets up part 2 in which I will flesh out the Cruciform Model of Inspiration and demonstrate how it transforms the Bible's problems into assets.

I begin in chapter 9 by critiquing Barth for failing to anchor his reflections on biblical inspiration in the cross. Chapters 10–14 then outline the Cruciform Model of Inspiration by discussing four overlapping aspects of the cross that I believe

12. My favorite is Meghan Good's *The Bible Unwrapped: Making Sense of Scripture Today* (Harrisonburg, VA: Herald, 2018). A classic in this field is G. Fee, D. Stuart, *How to Read the Bible for All It's Worth* (Grand Rapids: Zondervan, 2014 [1981]).

13. See M. J. Zia, *What Are They Saying bout Biblical Inspiration?* (Mahwah, NJ, Paulist Press, 2011). For a comprehensive historical overview and critique of various ways evangelicals have thought about biblical inspiration, see R. M. Price, *Inerrant the Wind: The Evangelical Crisis of Biblical Authority* (Amherst, NY: Prometheus Books, 2009).

should inform our thinking about biblical inspiration. Each one, I argue, helps us understand how the so-called problems of the Bible are not genuine problems. To the contrary, when understood in light of God's the cross, it becomes clear how these problems bear witness to the cross.

I will then bring this book to a close (save for a postscript) in chapter 15 by addressing the question of whether or not the Cruciform Model of Inspiration is consistent with Jesus's view, and treatment of, the OT.

* * *

My sincere prayer is that this book will help readers confidently embrace the divine inspiration of all Scripture and to see why this traditional belief is not threatened by historical-critical scholarship and the many problems in Scripture it has unearthed. Even more importantly, my prayer is that this book helps readers see how the crucified Christ permeates all of Scripture, including its errors, contradictions, inaccuracies, and morally offensive material.

PART I

Wrestling with "Problems"

1.

An Inconvenient Truth

> A finite point without an infinite reference point is essentially meaningless. —Jean Paul Sartre.

> Vanity of vanities, says the Teacher, vanity of vanities! All is vanity. . . . All things are wearisome, more than one can express; The eye is not satisfied with seeing, or the ear filled with hearing. What has been is what will be, and what has been done is what will be done. There is nothing new under the sun. —Ecclesiastes 1:1, 8–9

I hear that many readers skip introductions. If you skipped mine, I would strongly encourage you to read it before proceeding forward because this chapter presupposes some of what I shared there. As you (perhaps just now) know from the introduction, the church has traditionally considered the entire Bible to be God-breathed. In I will provide a defense of this perspective in chapter 3, but for now I'd like us to simply note that this conviction has been foundational to the life and faith of the church throughout history. Every reforming and reviving movement in church history was based on this foundation. Conversely, history has demonstrated that groups that abandon the church's traditional understanding of Scripture tend to drift outside the bounds of historic orthodox Christianity, as I noted in the introduction.

If we imagine the church as a ship on a tumultuous sea, the

Bible has always served as the rudder that keeps her on course. In our postmodern, post-Christendom, and (some are claiming) post-truth world, the sea in the Western world is as tumultuous as it has ever been. Which means, the Western church arguably has never needed its rudder more than it does right now.

* * *

Unfortunately, as badly as the church needs our revered rudder, we also need to acknowledge the inconvenient truth that our revered rudder contains some challenging material. My experience during my first semester at the U of M convinced me that this ancient collection of writings contains a multitude of errors, contradictions, and historical inaccuracies, as well as a good bit of morally offensive material, including a number of morally offensive depictions of God.

Before discussing this problematic material any further, however, I believe a preliminary pastoral word of caution is in order.

* * *

If you firmly believe that the Bible must be completely without error if it is to be considered to be divinely inspired, and if you've never before seriously wrestled with its problems, you should be forewarned that the following material could rattle your cage a bit. Believe me, I am *all too well* acquainted with how unsettling one's first encounter with the Bible's challenging material can be. And I'm going to shoot straight with you: I'm not going to pull any punches as I talk about this stuff. I am convinced that we can only begin to see why the so-called problems of the Bible aren't genuine problems if we stop trying to minimize or explain away these problems.

So, if you've always assumed that the Bible is inerrant, as I once did, and if this belief has been important to you, as it once was to me, this unflinching review of the Bible's problems may make you feel conflicted, angry, confused, and perhaps even a little scared. You may even feel like the foundation of your faith is crumbling.

If you begin to feel this way as you proceed, I want to encourage you to simply embrace those feelings. I'm sure you want to believe what is *true*, not simply what is convenient or what feels safe. And this means you have no choice but to wrestle with the inconvenient truth that the Bible we believe is entirely God-breathed contains material that doesn't conform to our commonsense assumptions about what a God-breathed book is *supposed to* look like.

As threatening as this material might initially be for some of you, I would ask you to bear in mind that we are working our way toward a cross-centered perspective that will actually *strengthen* your confidence in the plenary inspiration of Scripture by disclosing how these problems enhance, rather than detract from, this inspiration.

* * *

As I shared in the introduction, I enrolled in The Bible as Literature course at the U of M thinking it would be a cake-walk. That ridiculously naïve idea flew out the window about three seconds into our first class. "Critical scholars uniformly agree that Moses didn't write the Pentateuch," our professor confidently announced to open the first day of class. "By studying it critically," he continued, "scholars have determined that there are at least four different primary sources that editors later wove together." He was referring to the famous *Documentary Hypothesis*,* which, in one form or another, is embraced by the vast majority of *critical OT scholars** today.

My first instinct was to dismiss this multisource view of the Pentateuch as a piece of liberal propaganda. I knew that Jesus repeatedly referred to Moses as the author of the first five books of the Bible, as did several NT authors, and for me, that sufficed to settle the matter. For about twenty seconds.

Our professor proceeded to review some of the evidence that led OT scholars to this conclusion. I recall my anxiety level rising a bit higher with each new piece of evidence he presented. Why, for example, did the Genesis 1 creation account have such a different style, and even use a different word for *God*, than the Genesis 2 creation account? And why did these two accounts disagree on whether animals were created before or after humans?[1] Would Moses change writing styles, switch out different words for *God*, and contradict himself? That was my first encounter with the problems of the Bible. In the weeks that followed, I would be forced to confront numerous others.

To be clear, the course was not primarily focused on exposing the Bible's problematic material. It's stated purpose was to help us understand the Bible in its cultural context—though it seemed to me, and still seems to me, that this professor had a chip on his shoulder toward evangelical Christians. He never seemed to grow weary of exposing the ridiculousness of people who thought this problem-filled book was divinely inspired. In any event, as far as I was concerned, the course should have been titled The Bible's Many Problems.

What follows is a sampling of the sorts of problems I encountered in this course. I'll group them into four categories: (1) the manner in which the Bible reflects beliefs and practices that were common throughout the ANE; (2) the contradictions and common human errors found throughout the Bible; (3) archeological evidence that certain Bible stories are not grounded in history; and (4) morally offense material in the Bible, including morally offensive depictions of God.

* * *

First, it was very troubling for me to learn that the Bible was not the altogether unique book I had assumed it was. It turns out that much of the material in the OT has clear parallels in the literature of other nations in the *Ancient Near East (ANE)** where the Israelites were located. For example, the Babylonians had a creation story entitled *Enuma Elish*, which, in significant respects, is strikingly similar to the Bible's creation accounts. Everything starts in darkness. Creation happens in six days, followed by rest. A firmament is used to divide the waters above from the waters below. And, curiously enough, in both accounts light exists *before* the sun, moon and stars are even created.

1. Gen 1:24–27; cf. 2:7, 19.

Of course, there are significant differences between these two accounts as well. But the clear overlap between the accounts bothered me. If the Bible is the God-breathed story of God, I thought, shouldn't it reflect God's true perspective on how the world was created instead of reflecting an ancient and incorrect perspective that was shared by pagans?

Along the same lines, I learned that the OT consistently reflects the prescientific view of the cosmos that was common throughout the ANE. Like everyone else, the ancient Hebrews believed that the sky was a dome that was "hard as a molten mirror." [2] It had to be a firmament, for it held up water and kept it separated from the water below. This hard dome contained windows or floodgates that Yahweh would open to water the earth.[3]

Also, in accordance with commonplace beliefs of ANE, the Israelites believed this dome, as well as the earth, rested on pillars that were submerged in water that encompassed the earth.[4] This water, however, was not your typical H_2O. As was true throughout the ANE, the Israelites personified the water encompassing the earth as a menacing cosmic force, which is why we read a great deal about Yahweh rebuking this water and setting boundaries it cannot pass.[5] I was disturbed not only by the fact that the cosmology of the OT was so similar to the cosmologies of other ANE people, but even more that this perspective was *obviously wrong*.

I learned about many other parallels between the Bible and the literature of the ANE as well. Here is a small sampling:[6]

- Several ANE parallels to the Bible's flood story include a Noah-like figure who builds a huge boat to save his family as well as pairs of every kind of animal. Critical OT scholars generally concur that the ANE parallels are significantly older than the Genesis accounts.

2. Job 37:18; cf. Gen 1:7.
3. Gen 7:11; 8:2; Isa 24:18.
4. Ps 104:2–3, 5–6; cf. Job 9:6; 26:11; Ps 75:3.
5. Ps. 104:7; 77:16.
6. For a much more comprehensive discussion, see G. Boyd, *Crucifixion of the Warrior God: Interpreting the Old Testament's Violent Portraits of God in Light of the Cross*, 2 vols. (Minneapolis: Fortress, 2017), 1.746–60.

- Some of the laws in the OT are strikingly similar to the Babylonian *Code of Hammurabi*, which is several centuries older than the biblical material.
- All ANE groups had temples, priests, prophets, and a sacrificial system that closely resembled the ancient Israelites.
- Throughout the ANE we find that the relationship between people and a nation's chief god is centered on the nation's king, just as we find in the OT.
- Much of the imagery Israelites associated with Yahweh was standard fare throughout the ANE. Like other deities, for example, the Israelites believed Yahweh lived on a sacred mountain, rode down on thundering clouds, threw thunderbolts (lightning) as arrows, created wind by blowing air out of God's mouth, and enjoyed the sweet aroma of sacrificed animals which were offered to God as food.

If Israel was a uniquely chosen nation and the OT a uniquely God-breathed book, I wondered why so many of the Israelites' beliefs and practices were shared by other ANE people? In fact, critical Bible scholars concur that a significant amount of material in the OT appears to have been more or less taken directly from these other ANE sources.

* * *

A second group of problems concerned all the contradictions and mistakes that our professor delighted in pointing out to us. To give just a few examples:

- The author of 1 Samuel depicts *Yahweh* as inciting David to sin while the author of 2 Chronicles corrects him by claiming it was *Satan*, not Yahweh, that did the tempting.[7]

7. 1 Sam 24:1; 1 Chr 21:1.

- While some of the Bible's earlier material celebrates Yahweh as a God who visits "the iniquity of the parents upon the children . . . to the third and fourth generation," a later prophet depicts God as explicitly denying God does this. "The person who sins shall die," Ezekiel declares, adding that "a child shall not suffer for the iniquity of a parent."[8]
- The author of 2 Samuel says David paid fifty pieces of silver for Orman's threshing floor while the author of 1 Chronicles says he paid six hundred.[9]
- 2 Kings informs us that king Jehoiakim had a son named Jehiachin while Jeremiah recounts the Lord judging Jehoiakim by not giving him a son to reign after he died.[10]
- In Mark, Jesus claims Abiathar was high priest when David ate showbread in the temple, though, in fact, it was Ahimelec, Abiathar's father, who was high priest at this time.[11]
- Matthew mistakenly thought it was Jeremiah rather than Zechariah who talked about thirty pieces of silver being given to a potter (or, as Matthew has it, given for a potter's field).[12]

The list of similar contradictions and mistakes could be expanded into a sizeable volume. The vast majority of these are admittedly pretty trivial, but, to my great misfortune at the time, it only takes *one* demonstrable mistake or contradiction, however trivial, to demonstrate that the Bible is not altogether inerrant.

* * *

8. Ex 34:7; Nu 14:18; Deut 5:9; Ezek 18:20.
9. 2 Sam 24:24; 1 Chr 21:25.
10. 2 Kgs 24:6; Jere 36:30.
11. Mark 2:26.
12. Matt 27:9–10; cf. Zech 11:12–13.

Around the time I was running out of arguments in my evolutionary biology class, which I discussed in the introduction, my Bible as Literature professor introduced us to some of the Bible's historical inaccuracies, which constitute my third group of problems. Most of the twenty or so examples he reviewed didn't strike me as particularly compelling, largely because the available archeological evidence could be interpreted in different ways. But a few of his examples seemed undeniably persuasive.

For example, most critical OT scholars argue that archeological evidence suggests the Bible's account of Israel's exodus out of Egypt and conquest of the Promised Land is largely fictitious. The book of Joshua depicts the Israelites storming into Canaan and exterminating entire populations at the command of Yahweh and with the help of Yahweh. Unfortunately, OT scholars generally concur that the available archeological evidence indicates that the Israelites actually migrated into Canaan over several centuries, and with very little, if any, violence.[13] According to my professor in this class, the book of Joshua is nothing more than a piece of political propaganda that was composed hundreds of years after the events it purports to recount.

As I listened to my professor share these things, I recall feeling like the most precious thing I'd ever known was slipping away from me. All the dramatic experiences with God that I'd enjoy over the previous year were utterly useless as a vanguard against all the problems this professor was throwing at me.

* * *

The fourth and final group of problems that helped to decimate my year-old faith concerned what my professor called "the moral problems of the Bible." Looking back on it, I'm surprised that I had hardly noticed any of this disturbing material in my intense Bible reading throughout the previous year. I had read the entire Bible from cover to cover, because this is generally

13. See e.g., P. R. Davies, *In Search of "Ancient Israel": A Study in Biblical Origins* (New York: T&T Clark, 2015); N. P. Lemche, *The Old Testament between Theology and History: A Critical Survey* (Louisville: Westminster John Knox, 2008).

what was expected of all *true* disciples in my Pentecostal church. But I have to admit that there were parts of the Bible—rather large parts, actually—that I simply found too boring to read carefully.

On top of that, I suspect my reading of Scripture during the blissful year following my conversion reflected my confirmation bias, which is the universal human tendency to notice and maximize data that confirms our strongly held beliefs while minimizing, or overlooking altogether, data that conflicts with our strongly held beliefs. Throughout the previous year I had read the Bible with the strong belief that it was an altogether holy and inerrant book, and this belief undoubtedly caused me to instinctively minimize or completely overlook material that was not holy or not correct.

For example, I hadn't before noticed those passages in the Bible that require the death penalty for children who are lazy, rebellious, drunkards, or who strike their parents.[14] Nor had I noticed those passages that stipulate the death penalty for fornicators, adulterers, homosexuals, and for anyone who engaged in a number of other forbidden sexual relations.[15] And while stoning is the most common form of execution in the OT, our professor drew our attention to several passages that require offenders to be burned alive.[16]

How, I wondered, could an all-loving God possibly have inspired such cruel and primitive-sounding laws?

Not only this, but some of the Bible's capital crimes are for remarkably trivial offenses. A priest who didn't wash his hands properly before he entered the tent of meeting had to be stoned to death, as did anyone who so much as looked upon the tent's holy furnishings when they were covered![17] This was the same fate priests met if they entered the tent with their hair disheveled, their clothes torn, or after they had drunken any alcohol.[18] Similarly, execution was required for any person who engaged in any sort of work on the Sabbath. The simple act of lighting

14. Deut 21:18–21; Exod 21:15, 17; Lev 20:9.

15. E.g., Ps 59:5; Ps 83:17–18; Ps 109:13–15, 20.

16. Lev 20:14; 21:9.

17. Exod 19:12–13; Num 1:51; 3:38; 4:15, 20; 18:3, 22, 32.

18. Lev 10:6–10.

a candle or gathering sticks for firewood on the Sabbath would get a person stoned to death![19]

Could the Creator of heaven and earth really have been so nit-picky and austere?

Thankfully, capital punishment was not required if a woman accidentally touched a man's genitals in the process of trying to free her husband from a struggle with him. Similar to what we find in the previously mentioned *Code of Hammurabi*, however, this unfortunate lady had to have her offending hand cut off![20]

I had also missed how many vengeance-filled prayers are contained in the Bible, especially in the Psalms. While Jesus and Paul taught that we are to love our enemies, to forgive without limit, and to hope for the best for everyone, many Psalms express hatred toward enemies and pray their enemies are *never* forgiven.[21] Indeed, some psalmists explicitly ask Yahweh to "crush the heads" of their enemies, to "break the teeth in their mouths," to "let them vanish like water that flows away," or to blind or otherwise cripple their enemies.[22]

Some psalmists express their longing for vengeance in even more graphic terms. One psalmist asks Yahweh to melt his enemies like a slug in the desert heat and to make them like "a stillborn child that never sees the sun."[23] Another petitions Yahweh to make God's enemies "like tumbleweed" and to burn them up alive, while yet another hopes to see Yahweh "rain fiery coals," "burning sulfur," and a "scorching wind" down on his enemies.[24] In one particularly ghoulish passage, a psalmist goes so far as to relish the prospect of smashing the heads of his enemies' babies against rocks, while another goes so far as to pray that his enemies will "go down alive to the realm of the dead."[25]

He basically wants his enemies to be buried alive!

I had to admit to myself that, if I had come upon prayers

19. Exod 31:14, 35:2–3; Num 15:32–36; Lev 23:29–30.

20. Deut 25:12.

21. Matt 5:44–45; Luke 6:27–36; Rom 12:14–21; Luke 23:34; Matt 18:21–22; Ps 5:5; 59:5; 83:17–18.

22. Ps 139 :19, 68:21; Ps 58:6–7; Ps 69:23.

23. Ps 58 :8 ; Ps 11:6, cf. 140:10.

24. Ps 83:13–14, cf. 21:9.

25. Ps 137:9; Ps 55:15.

like this in any *other* religious book, I would certainly not have considered them to be divinely inspired. If anything, I might have suspected the most vicious of these prayers were demonically inspired. So, I wondered, is it not hypocritical of me to believe a hateful prayer is holy and divinely inspired when it's found in my Bible even though I would have considered this same prayer to be demonically inspired were it found anywhere outside the Bible?

* * *

Between the numerous biblical problems I confronted in my literature course and the compelling evidence for evolution I confronted in my biology class, my year-old fundamentalist faith didn't stand a chance. Several weeks before the semester ended, I felt I had no choice but to consciously renounce it. I can recall the exact moment like it happened yesterday.

I was sitting by myself in the next to last seat in a mostly empty shuttle bus that was driving U of M students to an offsite parking lot. It was a cold December, late Friday afternoon, and the overcast sky was just beginning to darken. I was nostalgically recalling some of the most powerful and joy-filled experiences I had enjoyed over the previous year. I remembered how absolutely certain I was at the time that I was experiencing the Holy Spirit. Not surprisingly, these experiences had come to a grinding halt as soon as I began questioning the Bible, and frankly, my heart ached for them.

What I missed even more, however, was that wonderful feeling of certainty I had enjoyed for almost a year, especially the certainty that my life had a purpose that would never ever end. I was now back to being certain of nothing, except that I could no longer embrace the Christian faith.

As I rested my head against the window, I saw in the distance the lot where I had parked. And for whatever reason, it was at that moment that I admitted to myself that I had lost all hope of salvaging my faith. My head tapped the window a few times as the shuttle went over a speed bump as it turned into my lot. As the shuttle slowed down, I knew I could no longer avoid the obvious, as much as I would have liked to. Just as the bus pulled to a full stop, I whispered to myself, "None of it was true."

As I stood up to exit the shuttle, everything felt surrealistic. The source and framework that had given meaning, purpose, and value to my life throughout the previous year was now gone. It felt like all color had suddenly been sucked out of the world. Everything felt cheap, trivial, shallow, and utterly insignificant. I was holding back tears as I stepped into the frigid Minnesota winter air.

The world had never before felt so cruel, cold, and dark.

2.

A Better Foundation

> I've read a great many novels and I know a fair amount about the legends that grew up among early people, and I know perfectly well the Gospel are not that kind of stuff. —C. S. Lewis

> We declare to you what was from the beginning, what we have heard, what we have seen with our eyes, what we have looked at and touched with our hands, concerning the word of life. —1 John 1:1

The nine months following my loss of faith were the darkest months of my life. If it was painful living in an absurd and pointless universe before my conversion, it was absolutely excruciating to return to this empty place after having spent a year feeling the opposite.

My existential anguish was made even worse because I felt like I was suffering alone. I missed the friends I had back in the Pentecostal church. The faith and experiences we shared had bound us closely together. I envied them for being able to continue to enjoy those experiences and close fellowship. It seemed like a delightful dream I almost wished I had not woken up from.

I had shared very little of the many devastating challenges I was encountering with my Pentecostal friends. It only made them defensive and suspicious of me. Plus, I frankly didn't see any point in possibly causing them to wake up from their comfortable dream and join me in the miserable meaningless void of reality. If everything is pointless, what difference does it make whether someone's beliefs are true or not if it makes them happy?

The only thing my Pentecostal friends knew was that I had come upon some unsolvable intellectual problems, which some interpreted to be an expression of my prideful trust in reason, while others suspected my intellectual problems were actually a subterfuge to conceal moral sin in my life. I didn't blame them for thinking this. It's what we all were indoctrinated into thinking.

Not only did I miss my former friends, I was having great trouble replacing them with new ones. I must have struck people as a gloomy, unfun person, but no one wanted to talk about the meaninglessness of existence, and I've frankly never been very good at making small talk, especially when consumed with heavy thoughts, as I was throughout this nine-month period.

The only companions I could find on the painfully godless journey I had embarked on were dead authors like Fredrick Nietzsche, Jean Paul Sartre, Albert Camus, and (my favorite) Francis Kafka.

Adding to my misery was the fact that I couldn't shake the memory of my dramatic encounters with God. I didn't just feel empty, as I did prior to my conversion. I now felt the painful *absence* of the joy, meaning, and psychological certainty I once had enjoyed. Nor could I entirely shake off my sense that these experiences had been genuine. I of course *tried* to explain them away as some sort of psychologically induced hysteria, but I did this only because I had no alternative, not because the explanation actually felt compelling.

I initially hoped my existential anguish would dissipate with time as I acclimated to the void I felt inside. The opposite happened. My solitary anguish intensified over the next nine months, to the point that it sometimes felt unbearable. I never seriously contemplated suicide, but as my despair deepened, I sensed I was heading in a direction where this could someday become conceivable. And that, frankly, scared the hell out of me!

Looking back, I believe the Spirit was doing a number of things at this point in my life to woo me back into a relationship with Christ, but it was this intensifying despair more than anything else that eventually opened me up to reconsider believing in Jesus—despite all the problems I knew were in the Bible.

* * *

It was either good luck, providence, or (as I'm inclined to suspect) a combination of the two that I met Frank around eight months into my miserable second-go-round with atheism.[1] Frank was a bright fellow philosophy major who was a year ahead of me in school. The reason I liked Frank was that he didn't mind me going on and on about the absurdity and meaninglessness of life in a Godless universe.

Not that Frank shared my nihilistic perspective. To the contrary, Frank turned out to be a passionate evangelical Christian who was planning on getting a PhD in philosophy or theology and becoming a professor. But, to his lasting credit, Frank was a really good listener, and he was able to empathize with my perspective without feeling the need to quickly "fix me" by cramming Jesus down my throat. Having someone who understood what I was talking about, and who patiently listened to what I had to say, alleviated my loneliness a little.

Most importantly, unlike other Christians I bumped into during my nine-month return-to-atheism phase, Frank didn't get defensive or preachy when I shared some of the problems that caused me to lose my faith, despite the fact that he didn't usually have a compelling response to them.

I had probably known Frank for around a month when he handed me a copy of *Mere Christianity*, by C. S. Lewis.[2] "If you want your decision to reject Jesus as Lord to be a fully informed decision," Frank said with a smile, "you really owe it to yourself to read this remarkable little book!" He then showed

1. With the exception of people who have given me permission to do otherwise, I have throughout this book altered the names of people, and, in several cases, the details of their stories, to preserve their anonymity.

2. C. S. Lewis, *Mere Christianity* (New York: Simon & Schuster, 1996 [1943]).

me a collection of essays by Lewis entitled *God in the Dock*, saying, "And when you're done with *Mere Christianity*, check out a couple of essays that I've marked out for you in this book."[3]

Before I could say anything, Frank handed me *God in the Dock* while explaining to me that Lewis was an Oxford professor of mythology and an atheist into his early thirties before coming to faith in Christ. And then, just for good measure, he handed me a third little book that Lewis wrote entitled, *Weight of Glory*, simply saying with a smile, "When you get around to it. These books," he said, "will help you understand why Lewis made that monumental decision."[4]

I assumed that an atheist Oxford professor wouldn't decide to become a Christian without good reason, so I took Frank's advice. I began reading *Mere Christianity* that night, and I was spellbound. The next day I parked myself in the coffee lounge of the U of M Library where I sat for the next fourteen hours, skipping two classes in the process. I finished *Mere Christianity* by midafternoon and then began plowing through *God in the Dock*. I did the same thing the following day, this time completing *God in the Dock* and then plowing through *Weight of Glory*, skipping three classes in the process.

Lewis was rocking my world! What I found most intriguing was that Lewis made a compelling case for believing in God and in Jesus *without appealing to the authority of the Bible*. Lewis's case for believing in God and Jesus was therefore completely unaffected by the Bible's many problems.

By the time I had finished these three books, I found I was, for the first time in nine months, beginning to have hope. Two of the arguments that I found in these books were particularly instrumental in rekindling my faith. What follows is a paraphrase of both arguments.

* * *

First, Lewis began to reconsider his atheism in favor of belief in God when he observed that nature only evolves creatures

3. C. S. Lewis, *God in the Dock* (Grand Rapids: Eerdmans, 1970).
4. C. S. Lewis, *Weight of Glory* (New York: HarperCollins, 1980 [1949]).

that crave things that nature itself can satisfy.[5] Creatures need to breathe, for example, and it just so happens that nature supplies them with air. And creatures need to eat, drink, and reproduce, and nature fortunately happens to provide them with food, water, and opportunities for sex. Imagine how unnatural it would be if nature evolved a creature that had a desperate need for something that nature itself couldn't provide.

When my wife Shelley was in her third trimester with each of our children, she would occasionally get a craving for a very specific food, usually for things like butterscotch, Oreo cookies, strawberries and whip cream, or pickles. When she was eight months pregnant with our third child, however, Shelley once developed an intense craving for something she couldn't quite identify. After she had spent a frustrating hour or so sampling different foods, she finally determined what it was.

Shelley was starving to death for some *radishes* with *peanut butter*!

This from a woman who had never before liked radishes! Now she craved them, with peanut butter, like an addict going through withdrawals! So, at quarter to ten in the evening, I was sent out with strict instructions not to return without at least two bags of radishes. (We already had peanut butter). I had to drive almost thirty miles to find a grocery store open that late, but my lovely pregnant wife was finally able to satisfy her highly idiosyncratic craving.

But imagine how strange and frustrating it would have been if Shelley had developed this intense craving for a food that didn't exist. And imagine how much more absurd it would have been if her craving for this nonexistent food wasn't just a momentary by-product of pregnancy-related hormone fluctuations but was rather a core aspect of her very identity. In this imaginary world, Shelley's whole life would be spent suffering a deep intense yearning for she-knows-not-what.

As painfully absurd as this scenario would be, it is not unlike the situation we find ourselves in, according to Lewis. Unlike animals, whose cravings and needs can be entirely met by

5. This argument is primarily derived from *Weight of Glory*, though it also is touched on in *Mere Christianity*.

nature, humans hunger for things that do not seem to exist in the natural world.

More specifically, humans are rational, purposeful, and moral agents. To one degree or another, we long to make rational sense out of our environment, to feel like our life has an ultimate point, and to see good triumph over evil. These are core aspects of what it means to be human. Yet, if the physical world is all that exists, then there is no ultimate reason, purpose, or moral value in nature. Hence, there is nothing in nature that corresponds to, let alone satisfies, these core longings.

Not only that, but Lewis observed that humans sometimes experience a profound longing for something we cannot put our finger on. It feels like nostalgia, but nostalgia for a place you can't seem to distinctly remember though you know you loved it, which is why you yearn for it now. Here again we find there is nothing in the natural world that can satisfy this yearning.[6] If the physical world is all that exists, and if *naturalistic** evolution tells the whole story about who human beings are and how we came about, then it seems that nature evolved creatures that are radically out of sync with itself.

Lewis concluded that the very fact that we have these yearnings suggests that there must be *something* beyond the natural world that corresponds to, and can potentially satisfy, these yearnings. And this *something*, Lewis eventually came to believe, must be a rational, purposeful, and morally supreme being. This *something*, in short, must be God.

In this light, Lewis held that our yearning can be understood as a sort of built-in homing device that is intended to lead us to a fulfilling relationship with our Creator. Lewis's argument hit close to home. Throughout my nine-month depressing journey into nihilism, I had wondered why it was so hard to live a meaningless and absurd life if it is in fact true that life is meaningless and absurd. How, I wondered, could simply knowing the truth make one so miserable? How could nature evolve a being that is so profoundly disappointed with it?

Lewis had not only provided me with an explanation for why

6. This yearning is frequently referred to by the German word *seinsucht*, which means "soft, wistful, tearful longing."

I was miserable as a nihilist: he had given me a hope that my core yearning might be eventually satisfied after all.

* * *

A second argument by Lewis affected me just as profoundly.[7]

As one of the world's leading experts on ancient mythology, Lewis noticed that the NT's story of God becoming a human, dying a sacrificial death, and rising from the dead, is echoed in some of the world's oldest and greatest mythology. Indeed, for a number of reasons, Lewis came to believe that the Christian Gospel was the greatest expression of this mythological motif. Unlike other myths, however, Lewis discovered that there were compelling historical reasons for believing that the Christian myth *actually happened*.

If you accept the *possibility* that the Gospel story *could* be historically true, he argued, the four Gospels give you just about every reason an ancient document could give you for believing they *are* true. This historical evidence, together with several other considerations, led Lewis to the conclusion that Jesus is "Myth become Fact."[8] Indeed, Lewis came to believe that, as fully God and fully human, Jesus was the reality to which all great mythology points.[9]

What impressed me most about Lewis's argument was that he appealed to reason and history, *not to a divinely inspired Bible*, when making his case for believing in Jesus. Yes, Lewis appealed to the Gospels, but he appealed to them not as divinely inspired documents but simply as ancient documents that need to be critically evaluated the same way historians critically evaluate other ancient documents.

This is precisely what allowed me to begin to once again consider embracing faith in Jesus, despite all the problems that I knew were in the Bible. Whatever else might be said about these

7. This argument is from *Mere Christianity*, though it is touch on in several essays in *God in the Dock* as well.

8. Lewis, *Weight of Glory*, 129.

9. *Weight of Glory*, 128–30. For a fuller discussion, see P. Eddy, G. Boyd, *The Jesus Legend: A Case for the Historical Reliability of the Synoptic Jesus Tradition* (Grand Rapids: Baker Academic, 2007), 160–62.

problems, they didn't substantially undermine the historical evaluation of the Gospels, and thus didn't undermine Lewis's case for believing that the historical Jesus was the Son of God, as the Gospels present him.

* * *

As I processed *Mere Christianity* and *God in the Dock* with Frank, I certainly hoped Lewis's case for believing in Jesus would stand up to scrutiny, and just having this hope alleviated much of my existential pain. But I had already experienced the anguish of losing my faith once, and I never wanted to go through anything like *that* again. This time, I had to be sure—at least as sure as anyone can be, given the nature of the evidence. Plus, I was aware that Lewis was not a critical NT scholar, and I wanted to know how experts evaluated the Gospels' historical veracity.

So, while Lewis's arguments marked a decisive turning point in my journey, I spent another six months or so reading just about every book I could find that addressed the question of the Gospel's historical reliability. I was surprised to find vast differences in the way various scholars interpreted the available evidence. Looking at the same four Gospels, I found scholars who argued that the Gospels are mostly fiction and that we can know next to nothing about the historical Jesus.[10] But I also found many other scholars, evangelical and otherwise, who argued that the Gospels provide us with an at least generally trustworthy portrait of the historical Jesus.[11]

It seemed to me at the time, as it still seems to me, that scholars arrive at such widely divergent interpretations of the available

10. Perhaps the most influence scholar who argued along these lines, and whom I read at as part of my study, is R. Bultmann, *The History of the Synoptic Tradition*, trans. J. Marsh (New York: Harper & Row, 1963). See also his *The New Testament and Mythology and Other Basic Writings*, trans. S. Ogden (Minneapolis, MN: Fortress, 1984).

11. A classic that I read at this time was F. F. Bruce, *The New Testament Documents: Are the Reliable?* (Grand Rapids: Eerdmans//Downers Grove, InterVarsity, 1981, [1943]. See also ch.1, fn.3. For a sampling of how differently scholars assess the evidence for the historical Jesus, see J. Beilby, P. Eddy, *The Historical Jesus: Five Views* (Downers Grove, IL: InterVarsity, 2009). For a contemporary assessment of the Synoptic Gospels and critical engagement with those who argue the Gospels are substantially legendary, see Eddy, Boyd, *Jesus Legend*.

evidence primarily because they approach this evidence with widely divergent assumptions. Many critical NT scholars assume that miracles don't ever happen. They therefore assume that any story containing a report of a miracle must be substantially, if not entirely, legendary.

Since the Gospels are filled with reports about Jesus's miraculous deeds, these scholars conclude that the Gospels must be substantially, if not entirely, legendary—notwithstanding how well these documents pass all the other standard tests for historical veracity that ancient documents are typically subjected to.

By contrast, I found that scholars who are open to the possibility of miracles tended to access the Gospels much more positively. And this is where I found myself. I had witnessed and heard about several apparent miracles in the Pentecostal church I had attended. I also had tried explaining my dramatic encounters with God away while I was in my nihilistic journey, but the truth was that each one of these felt miraculous, which is what made explaining them away so challenging.

I thus didn't have a problem being open to the possibility that reports of miracles could be factual.[12] Consequently, I found the arguments for the general reliability of the four Gospels to be more compelling than the arguments against their reliability.

Was my evaluation of the evidence influenced by the fact that I was in despair and *hoping* Lewis's claim about the Gospels' reliability would hold up under scrutiny? Of course it was! None of us thinks in a vacuum. In fact, science has recently demonstrated that our reason generally follows our heart (our intuitions, emotions, and desires) far more than it leads it.[13]

So yes, my evaluation of the available evidence was (and is) biased. But the very fact that we can become aware of our biases suffices as proof that we are capable of rational thinking. Moreover, the fact that I hoped the Gospels would prove reliable

12. I would soon discover that Lewis had written a strong defense of miracles. See C. S. Lewis, *Miracles* (New York: HarperCollins, 1974 [1947]. For a truly impressive collection of documented miracles, see C. Keener, *Miracles: The Credibility of the New Testament Accounts*, 2 vols. (Grand Rapids: Baker Academic, 2011).

13. See D. Kahnaman, *Thinking, Fast and Slow* (New York: Farrar, Straus & Giroux, 2011).

as I evaluated the evidence no more invalidates the arguments I would marshal in support of their reliability than it would invalidate arguments against their reliability if the person making this case had hoped the Gospels would prove unreliable when they evaluated the evidence.

* * *

There was a third, admittedly even more subjective, consideration that influenced my decision to return to faith, notwithstanding the Bible's problems. It had always seemed intuitively obvious to me, as I think it is to most psychologically healthy people, that if there is an ultimate purpose to life, it has to have something to do with love. And what is significant about this is that, undoubtedly influenced by Lewis, I had come to believe that the Gospel message is the greatest love story ever told, regardless of whether it is historical or not.

If we grant that the depth of a person's love can be measured by what they are willing to sacrifice for their beloved, then the love expressed in the Gospel story is beyond compare. This is a story of a God who, out of unfathomable love, was willing to go to the furthest extreme possible to rescue and restore a race of people who had made themselves God's enemies.[14] Out of love for us, the *holy* God went to the extreme of *becoming our sin*, and the *perfectly united* triune God went to the extreme of experiencing *separation from Godself*, as the Son of God bore the God-forsaken consequences that are intrinsic to sin.[15] Hence Jesus cried out on the cross, "My God, my God, why have you forsaken me?"[16]

In other words, out of love for us and the whole creation, God went to the extreme of becoming God's own antithesis! Which means that, in all eternity, God couldn't have gone further or couldn't have sacrificed more than God did on Calvary. And note this: the unsurpassable extremity to which God was willing to go on our behalf reveals the unsurpassable perfection of the love that God is, and the love that God has for us. This is

14. Rom 5:10; Eph 2:1, 5.
15. 2 Cor 5:21; Gal 3:13.
16. Mark 15:34.

precisely why the cross must be considered the unsurpassable revelation of God. No story could depict a lover sacrificing more, and for a beloved who could hardly have deserved it less.

I had thus come to believe that the Gospel story is the greatest expression of the purpose of life, if life in fact has a purpose. And, as we have seen C. S. Lewis argue, the very fact that I had a deep yearning for such a purpose suggests that such a purpose exists. Hence, on top of the reasons I had for thinking the Gospel story was anchored in "actual history," I also had this existential reason.

This story just fit. It had an intuitive ring of truth to it.

I eventually concluded that the Gospel story is the "true North" to which the compass of my heart, and I suspect every human heart, was pointing.

* * *

Primarily because of the three arguments I've just shared, I decided to recommit my life to Christ midway through my sophomore year at the U of M. Unlike my first conversion, this decision didn't involve a dramatic, emotional encounter with God. It was simply a calm and rational decision I made in the quiet of my bedroom—though, I should add, once I made it, the last vestiges of my existential pain were replaced by a sense of God's loving presence that I had missed so profoundly over the previous fifteen months.

Frank did not remain so calm, however. He had become something of a mentor to me over the previous six months as he patiently helped me slowly work my way back to the faith. Frank, who wasn't a particularly touchy-feely kind of guy, gave me an awkwardly long bear hug, and it was only when he pulled back to look into my eyes that I saw that his face was beaming and soaked with tears.

I didn't have a clue what to do with all the problems in the Bible when I came back to Christ. But my rekindled relationship with Jesus provided such a relief from my previous existential ache that I found I just wasn't all that concerned with them. Before long, however, I would discover that my caviler attitude toward the Bible's problems would prove unsustainable. Before I unpack the story of how I've wrestled with the Bible any further, however, I'd like to bring this chapter to a close by encouraging readers to consider structuring their faith in the way that I've outlined in this chapter.

* * *

Most Christians—certainly most evangelical Christians—believe in Jesus *because they first believe in the Bible*. As that old adage goes, "God said it, I believe it, that settles it for me." I strongly encourage you *not* to structure your faith that way. It was precisely because I based my faith in Jesus on my faith in the Bible that I lost my faith. I've seen many others tragically fall prey to the same unhelpful pattern.

I believe the Bible should play an irreplaceable role as the foundation for *what* Christians are to believe and for *how* Christians ought to live. As I said earlier, faith in the Bible's inspiration has served as the indispensable rudder of the church throughout history. But I'm afraid you are skating on very thin ice if you make the Bible the foundation for *why* you believe in Jesus in the first place. To state the matter in more precise philosophical terminology, I am claiming that the Bible should serve as the *theological*, but not the *epistemic*,* foundation of our faith.

As my own journey makes clear, the Bible simply cannot bear this weight.

It's got too many problems!

Instead, I encourage you to anchor your faith in Jesus based on the sorts of considerations I've reviewed in this chapter: namely, the demonstrably general reliability of the Gospels, the manner in which your innermost yearnings point in the direction of a God who alone can fulfill them, and the fact that the Gospel story is the greatest love story that could ever be told. Of course, you can't hope for certainty in such matters. But every time I've reexamined my reasons for believing Jesus is Lord, I have come away reconvinced that I have far more compelling reasons for concluding Jesus is Lord than for concluding he's not. And so, I have committed myself to thinking and living *as though* the Gospel message were true. This is simply what it means to walk by faith.

Look, we live each day *as though* many things were true, though we can't prove them. Which is to say, everyone walks by faith. If you don't think you walk by faith every time you get on a plane, for example, I encourage you to talk to a person with aviophobia (fear of flying). They'll remind you that you cannot *prove* that the plane you are about to board will not crash, for whatever reason. So, if you board that plane, you board by faith.

The aviophobic objection notwithstanding, it's very rational to act *as though* planes are safe, since you have far more reasons to believe the plane you're about to board will fly than you have for suspecting it will not. Similarly, I simply decided I have more reasons to live *as though* Jesus is Lord than I have for living *as though* he's not.

In any event, having this foundation solidly in place doesn't solve any of the Bible's problems. But it certainly removes some of the pressure to account for them. Your faith in Jesus is no longer on the line with every error, contradiction, inaccuracy or morally offense story or portrait of God that you come across in the Bible.

However, as we'll see in the following chapter, this is not to suggest that we don't have *other* important reasons for trying to make sense of the Bible's many problems.

3.

Between Scylla and Charybdis

> When you're between a rock and a hard place, it won't be a dead end—Because I am God, your personal God, The Holy of Israel, your Savior. —Isa 43:2–4 (The Message)

> Scylla and Charybdis in Greek Mythology: two immortal and irresistible monsters who beset the narrow waters traversed by the hero Odysseus in his wanderings described in Homer's *Odyssey*. . . . To be "between Scylla and Charybdis" means to be caught between two equally unpleasant alternatives.—Encyclopedia Britannica

I was glad my new-found faith in Jesus was immune to the Bible's many problems, but on some level, I knew that I couldn't sustain my ambivalence about the Bible's inspiration indefinitely. Sooner or later, I would have to figure out what I thought about the Bible and its problems, especially since I began to feel called to be a teacher or preacher soon after I recovered my faith in Christ.

An opportunity to reopen the issue presented itself midway through my junior year, roughly a year after I'd rededicated my life to Christ. The problems posed by the Bible resurfaced for me not out of a concern for biblical authority, but out of a conundrum I found myself in concerning Jesus's authority.

* * *

I continued to avidly read the Bible once I came back to Christ, despite the fact that I still had no clue what to do with its many problems. While I embraced no theory of inspiration at this point in my life, I often felt that reading the Bible and hearing it preached helped me connect with God, and it had a positive spiritual influence on my life, at least so long as I could push its problems out of mind. On a strictly experiential and intuitive level, I knew that the Bible had to be, in some sense, divinely inspired, notwithstanding its many problems.

One evening while reading the Bible, I came upon Jesus's debate with the Pharisees in John 5. At one point Jesus said to these men: "You search the scriptures because you think that in them you have eternal life; and it is they that testify on my behalf." Jesus then concluded his argument by telling them: "If you believed Moses, you would believe me, for he wrote about me. But if you do not believe what he wrote, how will you believe what I say?"[1]

What struck me most about this remarkable teaching on this particular evening was that Jesus associated people believing in Moses with people believing in Jesus's own Lordship. As I contemplated this, it occurred to me that the logic of Jesus's teaching worked the other way around as well. If believing Moses should lead to believing in Jesus, then shouldn't believing in Jesus lead to believing Moses? For Jesus clearly not only believed Moses; he believed Moses's writings were *all about himself.*

And with this thought, I found myself in an intellectual conundrum, one that I wouldn't manage to free myself from for the next six years. On the one hand, I had all my reasons for believing Jesus was Lord, as I discussed in the previous chapter. On the other hand, however, I didn't see how believing Moses was a viable option, given all the evidence I'd seen that the *Pentateuch** was a compilation of multiple sources and oral traditions that were compiled and *redacted** over a long period of time. Moreover, even apart from that issue, I remained keenly aware that the Pentateuch, as well as the rest of the Bible,

1. John 5:39–40, 46–47.

contained errors, contradictions, inaccuracies, and morally offensive material.

I found myself caught between the Charybdis of denying Jesus's authority and the Scylla of undeniable problems in the Bible.

* * *

The Gospel of John obviously gives a more theologized portrait of Jesus than the three *Synoptic Gospels*,* but from my six-month study of the Gospels, mentioned in the previous chapter, I felt quite confident that John's portrait of Jesus was generally reflective of the historical Jesus. But I didn't at this point have any reason to believe that he or any other biblical author was infallible. It was, therefore, possible that John's depiction of Jesus in this passage reflected more of John's theology than that of the historical Jesus. I thus decided to cast a broader net by studying what the other Gospels had to say about Jesus's beliefs about Moses and the OT in general.

My research soon led me to an old collection of essays by a Princeton Seminary professor named Benjamin B. Warfield, entitled *The Inspiration and Authority of the Bible*.[2] I was rather surprised by what I discovered. Warfield demonstrated that Jesus and the authors of the NT shared at least the general features of the conventional first century Jewish assumption that the entire OT is divinely inspired and is therefore completely trustworthy. Among other things, Warfield demonstrates that Jesus, as well as certain NT authors, use "Scripture says" and "God says" interchangeably. So closely do they associate God and Scripture that they occasionally even ascribe divine attributes—such as divine foreknowledge—to Scripture.[3] I was also impressed by Warfield's demonstration of how often, and how emphatically, Jesus and certain NT authors cite biblical verses and biblical stories. And when Jesus and the authors of the NT say, "It is written," which Warfield demonstrates they do quite frequently,

2. B. B. Warfield, *The Inspiration and Authority of the Bible* (Philadelphia, PA: Presbyterian and Reformed, 1970 [1948]). What follows is from pages 245–407.

3. Gal 3:8.

it is clear they are appealing to writings they believe carry unquestionable divine authority.

I was similarly impressed with how frequently Jesus and certain NT authors insist that everything in Scripture, down to its last letter and even "stroke of a letter," had to be fulfilled in Jesus's life, ministry, death and resurrection.[4] In fact, while I didn't fully appreciate it at the time, I've since come to see how thoroughly the OT permeates Jesus's theology, mission, and even his own self-understanding.[5]

I was forced to face this dilemma: If I confess Jesus to be Lord, I don't see how I can possibly reserve for myself the right to correct his theology, especially on such a foundational matter. Sure, as a full human being, Jesus would have shared the general worldview assumptions of his first-century Jewish Palestinian culture. And this means Jesus could be mistaken about things. He probably really believed the mustard seed was the smallest of all seeds, for example.[6] On the other hand, Jesus never claimed to *teach* anything he hadn't heard directly from his Father, and all four Gospels agree that he explicitly taught that the OT was the divinely inspired story of God.[7]

At the same time, I couldn't see how I could, with intellectual integrity, embrace Jesus's perspective, owing to all the problems I was all too well aware of. Like I said, I was caught between the impossible Charybdis of denying Jesus's authority and the equally impossible Scylla of denying that the OT is filled with problems.

I was also aware of certain problems with the NT as well, such as the assortment of contradictions that exist between the four Gospels. For example, did Jesus say the rooster would crow once after Peter's three denials of Jesus, as Matthew, Luke and John recount, or twice, as Mark recounts it?[8] Or, did Jesus cleanse the temple at the beginning of his ministry, as John recounts, or at the very end of his ministry, as the Synoptic Gospels claim?[9]

4. Matt 5:17–18.
5. See B. Witherington III, *The Christology of Jesus* (Minneapolis: Fortress, 1990).
6. Matt 13:31–32.
7. John 5:19–20; 30. Cf. John 3:32; 8:26; 14:19, 24; 15:15.
8. Matt 26:34; Luke 22:34, John 13:38; Mark 14:30.
9. John 2:13–16; Matt 21:12–13; Mark 11:15–17; Luke 19:45–46.

There are a multitude of apparent or real contradictions like this between the Gospels.

These contradictions are all on minor matters, however, and I had already learned that minor contradictions over details is to be expected whenever multiple witnesses report on the same event. As such, I didn't feel that these contradictions did much to undermine the substantial reliability of the Gospels. But while these discrepancies posed no significant challenge to the historical-critical evaluation of the Gospels, it seemed to me that they posed an enormous challenge to the belief that these documents are God-breathed. You expect human witnesses to contradict each other at points, but you wouldn't expect this of a book that was breathed by the Creator of heaven and earth. Or so I assumed at the time.

I thus wondered if my Charybdis and Scylla conundrum extended into the NT as well. I spent some time looking into whether or not Jesus had ever said anything about the NT that might suggest he viewed it as being on a par with the OT.

* * *

Frankly, I couldn't find much, which is hardly surprising since none of the books of the NT were written until decades after Jesus lived. But I did come upon a few statements I thought might be relevant, especially in the Gospel of John. For example, Jesus promised his disciples that the Holy Spirit "will teach you everything, and remind you of all that I have said to you."[10] Later he told them, "I still have many things to teach you, but you cannot bear them now. When the Spirit of truth comes, he will guide you into all the truth."[11]

Of course, Jesus may have only been claiming that his disciples' preaching would be Spirit-inspired, but I saw no reason why this promise couldn't apply to their future writings as well, especially if Jesus anticipated that the nations of the world would not be reached with the Gospel within his disciples' lifetimes. Obviously, the only way that the disciple's reports on Jesus's deeds and teachings could be received after their deaths

10. John 14:26.
11. John 16:12–13.

would be by being written down, and John, at least, tells us he wrote his Gospel "so that you may come to believe that Jesus is the Messiah, the Son of God."[12]

On the other hand, from my studies I had learned that many NT scholars argue that Jesus and the earliest disciples believed history would come to an end either during or shortly after Jesus's ministry, in which case it's less likely that Jesus envisioned his disciples putting their Gospel message into written form.[13]

This is generally referred to as "the apocalyptic view of Jesus." At the same time, it seemed to me (and still seems to me) that the very fact that we're learning about Jesus's promise of the Spirit's future inspiration through a written Gospel suggests that John at least believed this promise included his written Gospel.

I have since found another consideration that argues against the apocalyptic view of Jesus. Those who espouse the apocalyptic view of Jesus assume that when Jesus spoke of wars, earthquakes, famines, persecutions, and the return of the Son of Man all taking place before his generation passed away, he was mistakenly predicting the soon-approaching end of the world.[14] While this language might sound to us like this to us, N. T. Wright has made a forceful case that Jesus was actually employing well-known apocalyptic imagery that no one in his audience would have interpreted literally. It was simply a powerful way of communicating that "the world as you know it is about to come to an end."[15]

According to Wright, as well as a number of other scholars, for first century Palestinian Jews, the end-of-the-world-as-you-know-it event that Jesus was talking about came in 70 CE with the destruction of the temple and the expulsion of the Jews from Jerusalem. According to most of these scholars, while Paul and other NT authors yet looked forward to the return of Jesus and the full establishment of his eternal kingdom on earth, most of

12. John 20:31.

13. A classic work reflecting this perspective is A. Schweitzer, *The Quest of the Historical Jesus*, trans. W. Montgomery (Mineola, NY: Dover, 2005 [1911]).

14. Matt 24:1–31.

15. N. T. Wright, *The New Testament and the People of God* (Minneapolis: Fortress, 1992), 333 (emphasis in text).

Jesus's and Paul's graphic language of an impending judgment relates to this tragic event, not to the end of history.

Hence, when Jesus suggests that the world would come to believe in him through the preaching of his disciples, there is no reason to assume Jesus thought this would happen in one generation, and hence no reason not to apply his promise of the Spirit's inspiration to their future writings.

* * *

Of course, while my confidence in the general reliability of the Gospels inclined me to trust that Jesus's promises about the Spirit went back to the historical Jesus, I also knew I had no way to prove this. And I was aware that some critical NT scholars argue that this and any number of other alleged teachings of Jesus in the Gospels actually originated in the early church and were then retroactively put into the mouth of Jesus. I have since learned that there are a number of formidable objections that can be raised against this proposal, but I didn't know these objections at the time.[16] As a result, I didn't feel like I could put much weight on those passages in which Jesus promised his disciples that the Holy Spirit would inspire their teachings, especially since they are all found in John who, as I said earlier, presents a more theologized portrait of Jesus than the Synoptics.

Around this same time, however, I was struck with a different consideration that seemed to provide a more persuasive reason for granting the NT the same divine authority that Jesus ascribes to the OT.

* * *

The OT that Jesus endorses tells the story of the Creator God working to raise up a nation of covenant partners in order to serve as the means by which God reunites and reconciles the entire world to Godself. It is the result of the Spirit inspiring people to interpret and bear witness to God's mighty deeds in history so as to provide the foundational narrative that shapes

16. See P. Eddy and G. Boyd, *The Jesus Legend: A Case for the Historical Reliability of the Synoptic Tradition* (Grand Rapids: Baker Academic, 2007), 269–308.

the communal identity of God's people as representatives of this God and as called-out missionaries to the world. Were it not for these writings, we would never have known about God's call to Abraham, the deliverance of God's people out of Egypt, God's ongoing struggles with Israel, or any of the other things found in God's inspired story in the OT.

In this light, I surmised, it would be exceedingly odd if God abruptly discontinued this pattern just prior to accomplishing God's greatest deed in history, in the person of Jesus Christ, especially since Jesus's early disciples understood him to be the fulfillment of the OT. If the communal identity of God's people required inspired recollections and interpretations of God's activity in the long period leading up to Christ, how could God's people *not* need this after the coming of Christ? The earliest Christians seem to have intuited this, for they almost immediately began to confer on the writings that came to comprise the NT the same divine authority they ascribed to the OT. Indeed, even within the NT we find Peter already referring to Paul's writings as "scripture."[17]

The very fact that the church has always placed the NT alongside the OT and confessed both to be "God-breathed" seems to me to be a further compelling reason for accepting the inspiration of the NT. For Jesus had promised that he would remain in the community of God's people to help with their decision-making.[18] I don't believe this implies that the church tradition always got things right, for as I will argue later on, the Spirit always works by means of a loving i*nfluence* rather than by *coercion*. But we're talking about a conviction that, until very recently, has been uniformly held by Christians and that has served as the bedrock for the church's identity, faith, and ethic throughout history, as I said in chapter 1.

I, for one, found it hard not to believe the Spirit was at

17. 2 Peter 1:15–16. I should note that, primarily because the style and vocabulary of 2 Peter differs significantly from 1 Peter, many NT scholars argue it is a pseudonymous work. Alternatively, Peter many have relied on an *amanuensis** who transposed his teachings in their own terms.

18. Matt 18:19–20; Matt 28:20. Interesting, after leaders in Jerusalem resolved a pressing dispute, the prefaced their conclusion by saying, "it seemed good to the Holy Spirit and to us" (Acts 15:28).

work when the church embraced the entire Bible as the inspired story of God. Not only that, but as I mentioned earlier, I often experienced the Spirit at work when reading the Bible or hearing it preached, something that holds true for countless Christians throughout history. Thus, on the authority of Jesus, his church, as well as my own experience, I felt, and still feel, compelled to accept the full inspiration of both the Old and New Testaments.

And yet, I still didn't have a clue how I could avoid Charybdis without being devoured by Scylla.

4.

Taking Another Look

It is a capital mistake to theorize before one has data. Insensibly one begins to twist facts to suit theories, instead of theories to suit facts. —Sir Arthur Conan Doyle (Sherlock Holmes)

Desire without knowledge is not good, and one who moves to hurriedly misses the way. —Proverbs 19:2

Frank and I continued to discuss theology every now and then over the next year, though it was challenging since Frank graduated at the end of my Junior year and was now enrolled full time in a local evangelical Seminary.

Like most evangelicals, at least back in the late 1970s, Frank was a strong believer in the inerrancy of the Bible. Yet, since my recommitment to Christ, we hadn't discussed the Bible's problems all that much. Our focus instead had been on the reasonableness of believing that the historical Jesus was God incarnate and responding to scholars like John Hick who had recently edited and published a highly controversial book entitled *The Myth of God Incarnate*.[1]

The focus of our discussions changed quickly, however, once I shared my conundrum with Frank. For the next several

1. John Hick, ed., *The Myth of God Incarnate* (Philadelphia: Westminster, 1977). For critical responses to this volume, see Michael Green, ed., *The Truth of God Incarnate* (Grand Rapids: Eerdmans, 1977); Alasdair Heron, "Article Review: Doing Away with the Incarnation?," *Scottish Journal of Theology* 31 (1978) 51–57.

months, our discussions revolved around biblical inerrancy. It wasn't only my conundrum that motivated our prolonged discussions. This was 1978, back when the battle over biblical inerrancy was hitting a fever-pitch among American evangelicals. In fact, Frank had already been in discussions on this topic with several concerned fellow Seminarians.

We were about to enter this fever-pitch for ourselves.

* * *

Frank contended that the doctrine of biblical inerrancy was implicit in the teachings of Jesus, appealing, for example, to Jesus's teaching that "scripture cannot be broken" and that not even a single "jot or tittle" in the law would pass away "until everything is accomplished."[2] Not only this, but as holds true for many evangelicals, Frank was convinced that biblical inerrancy necessarily followed from a belief in God's perfection. "To admit that the Bible contains errors," he once told me, "is tantamount to saying that a perfect God inspired an imperfect book, which," he insisted, "is an utterly incoherent supposition."

Frank also espoused the common evangelical conviction that the doctrine of biblical inerrancy was absolutely essential for the safeguarding of orthodoxy. "If we have to figure out what is and is not true in Scripture," he argued, "then human reasoning, rather than the Bible, is the ultimate authority in our life. And the thing about human reason," Frank added, "is that its fallen and self-serving. If reason is in charge, then everyone will end up choosing which parts of the Bible they want to believe based on little more than their own subjective preferences."

I was very sympathetic to Frank's concerns. In fact, I could discern only one flaw in his reasoning. "You make a great case for the Bible we both *wish* we had," I told Frank, "but it seems to me that your arguments fly in the face of the Bible we *actually* have. For it is an indisputable fact that the Bible we *actually* have is not a perfect, errorless book." I then illustrated my point by sharing several examples of the material I covered in chapter 1. Frank responded by insisting that all the problems in the Bible

2. John 10; 38; Matt 5:17–18.

were superficial. He was convinced that, if we dug deep enough, most if not all of these alleged problems could be explained away.

I respected Frank a great deal, and I honestly *wanted* to believe he was right. Among other things, this struck me as the only way out of my conundrum. But I nevertheless had to admit to Frank that I was highly skeptical of his claim.

Frank, who never flinched in the face of tough questions, responded by suggesting we openly investigate the matter. He proposed that he and I, along with several fellow seminarian friends who were passionate about this topic, form a study group. Our goal would be to determine to what degree the alleged errors, contradictions, historical inaccuracies, and morally offensive material of the Bible could be plausibly explained away.

Over the last three months of my Junior year, this group, made up of six guys alongside Frank and myself, would meet every Thursday evening in a Minneapolis café for two to three hours. Each week, I (and occasionally one or two others) would bring a dozen or so problems that we had come upon, and throughout the ensuing week each of us would devote whatever available time we had to investigating ways of solving each of these problems. Everyone would then share their findings the next time we met.

Altogether, we ended up discussing about a hundred and twenty of the Bible's problems. The vast majority of these were trivial—they didn't affect the Bible's central storyline and message. What difference does it really make, for example, that Matthew mistakenly thought it was Jeremiah rather than Zechariah who talked about thirty pieces of silver?[3] And who really cares whether the author of 2 Kings was right in claiming that King Jehoiakim had a son who succeed him on the throne or if Jeremiah was right in claiming Yahweh prevented this from happening?[4] But this is precisely what makes the doctrine of biblical inerrancy so vulnerable and so dangerous for people to hold! For as I said in chapter 1, it only takes one demonstrable

3. Matt 27:9; cf. Zech: 11:12–13.

4. 2 Kgs 24:6; cf. Jer 36:30.

imperfection, however trivial, to destroy this belief, and all too often, the Bible-dependent faith of the person who holds to it.

* * *

In the final meeting of this inerrancy study group, each participant shared their perspective on how successful they felt we had been at finding plausible resolutions to the problems we had addressed. I and two other participants estimated our success rate significantly lower than the other five. One major reason for our differences was that, unlike the other five participants, we didn't think it was valid to try to explain away a biblical problem by arguing that it didn't exist in the original autographs but instead crept into the text sometime later on as manuscripts were being copied by scribes.

There is no denying that scribes reproduced manuscripts imperfectly. By comparing ancient manuscripts, *textual critics** seek to locate when and where mistakes were introduced into the textual tradition. In this way these scholars help us get closer to the original autographs. Now, if there is actual *textual evidence* that a mistake or contradiction arose in the process of reproducing manuscripts, then it is of course perfectly acceptable to appeal to this. For example, it is well-known that the last nine verses of Mark's Gospel are not in the earliest manuscripts. These verses contain several potentially problematic teachings such as requiring baptism for salvation and the claim that disciples won't be harmed if they are bitten by poisonous snakes or drink poison.[5] In this case, I think it is legitimate to respond to these problematic teachings by pointing out that it's highly unlikely they were part of Mark's original Gospel.

But this wasn't the case for the majority of the problems this group was trying to explain away. And since the original autographs of the biblical writings are not available, my two more skeptical friends and I felt that claiming these autographs lacked a problem that is in our current Bible was weak, to say the least.

The three of us also seemed to have a higher standard for

5. Mark 16:9–10.

plausibility than the other five members of our study group. For example, at one point, our group discussed the above-mentioned contradiction between 2 Kings and Jeremiah regarding whether or not King Jehoiakim had an heir to the throne. Without any supporting evidence, one participant suggested that God must have changed God's mind sometime after God had announced that Jehoiakim would have no heir. While the other five members of our group thought this fellow's explanation was plausible, I and my two more skeptical comrades considered it an act of desperation.

Still, even Frank, the most ardent defender of inerrancy in our group, conceded that at least over a quarter of the problems we examined remain unresolved. I and my two more-skeptical colleagues felt this was true for at least half of the problems we examined. However you cut it, that's a lot of unresolved problems, and there are hundreds and hundreds more where those came from! At what point, I asked Frank, do you just abandon the inerrancy ship?

Wherever that point is, I and my two more skeptical friends were pretty sure we had crossed it.

* * *

Our inability to resolve so many of the Bible's problems wasn't the only shortcoming of our three-month study group, in my opinion.[6] While I never shared this with the rest of the group, at some point I began to feel like there was something disingenuous about the way we were going about things. We weren't trying to assess the Bible's problems in an honest and objective manner. Nor were we trying to follow the facts wherever they might lead, which is what I thought you were supposed to do if you were on a serious quest for truth.

We were instead only looking for support for what we already believed, or at least *wanted* to believe. When each of us reported possible solutions to the problems we had worked on in the previous week, we almost always cited conservative evangelical

6. One major shortcoming that is painfully obvious to me now but that we were incognizant of in 1978 was that our group was comprised exclusively of well-educated middle-to-upper-middle class white American males.

authors who were themselves defenders of inerrancy. Not only this, but toward the end of our study, I began to suspect that there was something duplicitous in my own approach to Scripture. As mentioned in chapter 2, I was more than happy to employ a historical-critical approach to the Gospels to make the case that Jesus Christ is Lord. Yet, many of the solutions that this group proposed where predicated on the delegitimization of the historical-critical method.[7]

For example, one of the first problems we attempted to tackle was an apparent contradiction between Genesis 1 and 2. As I noted in chapter 1, the first says humans were created *after* God created animals while the second depicts Adam being created *before* the animals.[8] Almost all historical-critical scholars concur that this contradiction, together with a number of other considerations, are evidence that these two chapters contain two originally independent creation accounts. Well, rather than considering the possibility that this historical-critical perspective of these two chapters might be correct, this inerrancy study group just assumed this perspective was an illegitimate means of explaining this contradiction because granting this much would undermine inerrancy.

I eventually came to see that I was rather hypocritically accepting the historical-critical approach to Scripture when it was advantageous to my faith while denying its legitimacy when it wasn't. Not exactly what you'd call methodological consistency.

Finally, as we poured over these problems week after week in our futile attempt to salvage inerrancy, it began to feel to me like we were trying to move Mount Everest with a tablespoon. If the doctrine of biblical inerrancy is so important, I thought, why should it take such a Herculean effort—let alone such a *futile* Herculean effort—to defend it? Or, to pose my question from

7. To be clear, my appreciation of a historical-critical approach to the Bible should not be taken to mean that I adopt the naturalistic presuppositions that have so often accompanied this method. Along with Paul Eddy, I have instead argued for an "open historical-critical method," i.e., one that relies on a historical-critical methodology but that is open to the possibility of God working miraculously in history. See Eddy and Boyd, *Jesus Legend*, ch. 1.

8. Gen 1:28–29; 2:7, 18–19.

the opposite direction: If the Spirit of the all-mighty God had "inerrancy" as one of her goals in "breathing" sacred Scripture, how could she have failed so spectacularly?

* * *

At the close of our last meeting, Frank professed that he continued to believe in the Bible's inerrancy, despite its numerous unresolved problems. He said he'd rather hold fast to Jesus's authority and live with unresolved problems than to disagree with Jesus on the basis of these problems. Plus, he felt that abandoning inerrancy would be disastrous for the church in the long run. The other four more conservative members of our group expressed their general agreement with Frank.

While I and my two more skeptical comrades certainly didn't want to disagree with Jesus, we also were inclined to believe that the unresolved problems were fatal to the doctrine of inerrancy. I reassured Frank that, on the authority of Christ, the church tradition, and my own experience, I still believed the Bible was, in some very important sense, God-breathed. But I also told him that, whatever other conclusions might be entailed by belief in the Bible's inspiration, our three-month study had convinced me that the total inerrancy of the Bible could not be considered one of them.

Which meant that Frank was pretty certain I was heading down a slippery slope toward liberalism, and I found myself still caught between the same old Charybdis and Scylla.

5.

Searching for a Safe Zone

> The most fearless hearts, the audacious dreamers, have always maintained a sense of optimism in the face of the available evidence. —Martin O'Malley

> Search, and you will find. —Matthew 7:7

I continued to wrestle with my conundrum on and off over the next six years. If I found a book or academic article that held to anything close to the traditional view of biblical authority while addressing its many problems, I read it. My reading included a number of evangelical authors who openly acknowledged the Bible's unresolved problems but who nevertheless tried to defend a limited or qualified concept of biblical inerrancy.[1]

Some argued that biblical authors were without error in matters of doctrine and morals, but not necessarily in matters of history and science.[2] Others argued that the biblical authors were inerrant in terms of what they explicitly taught, but not

1. For an excellent overview of the evangelical options while defending limited inerrancy, see S. T. Davis, *The Debate About the Bible* (Philadelphia: Westminster, 1977). For a comprehensive, critical, and insightful historic overview of evangelical strategies for preserving some concept of inerrancy, see R. M. Price, *Inerrant the Wind: The Evangelical Crisis of Biblical Authority* (Amherst New York: Prometheus Books, 2009).

2. E.g., D. M. Beegle, *The Inspiration of Scripture* (Philadelphia, PA: Westminster, 1963); J. Rogers, *Confessions of a Conservative Evangelical* (Philadelphia, PA: Westminster, 1974).

in terms of the ancient, fallible, and culturally conditioned way they communicated these inerrant teachings.[3]

Similarly, I found a number of authors who argued that the Bible's inerrancy was defensible when assessed by ancient rather than modern standards. They noted, for example, that ancient historians were generally less interested in providing a completely accurate, factual account of the past than they were in drawing out moral or political lessons for the present.[4] They thus operated with a much looser sense of historical accuracy than contemporary historians. Hence, these scholars argued, a biblical narrative should not be considered erroneous simply because it doesn't meet contemporary standards for historical accuracy.[5]

Some within this group applied a similar line of reasoning to account for Jesus's reference to Moses as the author of the Pentateuch. They contend that we're anachronistically reading contemporary Western concerns into Jesus's words if we think these references require us to believe that Moses alone wrote the Pentateuch. Jesus was using the linguistic conventions of his day, not preauthorizing an answer to our contemporary historical-critical questions.

I also found some authors within the broad tent of evangelicalism who tried to safeguard the Bible's inerrancy by restricting it to material that pertained to our salvation, while others went even further by limiting inerrancy to the central message of the Bible, though I could find no consensus on what exactly this inerrant central message was.[6] It lies outside

3. E.g., B. Ramm, *The Christian View of Science and Scripture* (Grand Rapids: Eerdmans, 1974); C. Pinnock, *A Defense of Biblical Infallibility* (Nutley, NJ: Presbyterian & Reformed, 1975; J. R. Michaels, "Inerrancy or Verbal Inspiration? An Evangelical Dilemma," in *Inerrancy and Common Sense,* ed. R. R. Nicole and J. R. Michaels (Grand Rapids: Baker, 1980).

4. E.g., J. J. Davis, "Genesis, Inerrancy and the Antiquity of Man," in *Inerrancy and Common Sense*, 137–59; J. I. Packer, *Fundamentalism and the Word of God* (Grand Rapids: Eerdmans, 1970); K Koch, *The Growth of the Biblical Tradition* (New York: Scribner, 1969).

5. I will use cautionary quotes when referring to "actual history" to remind readers that what we call "actual history" is always someone's theoretical reconstruction of what they *believe* actually happened. Every version of "actual history" is thus influenced by the biases of the person who reconstructed it.

6. E.g., G. C. Berkouwer, *Holy Scripture,* trans. J. Rogers (Grand Rapids: Eerd-

the scope of this book to enter into a detailed discussion of the merits and shortcomings of each of these proposals. Three general comments must suffice.

First, I found a wealth of valid insights in many of these positions. For example, to this day I believe it is extremely important to distinguish between the God-intended revelatory message that God breathed through an author, on the one hand, and the fallible and culturally conditioned way the author expressed that message, on the other. Indeed, we'll later see that the Cruciform Model of Inspiration accentuates the importance of this distinction.

Moreover, I firmly believe Scripture should be assessed by ancient rather than modern standards. When these sorts of qualifications are made, I continue to be impressed with how well the Bible, on the whole, stands up to critical scrutiny, as I mentioned in chapter 1. Which is to say, I tend to be more often persuaded by arguments defending the basic historicity (by ancient standards) of biblical accounts than by arguments that deny this.[7]

Second, as helpful and clarifying as some of these inerrancy-qualifying proposals were, I had reservations about some of the categories these authors imposed on Scripture. For example, I found it (and continue to find it) challenging to draw a hard and fast distinction between Scripture's doctrinal, ethical, or salvific material, on the one hand, and its historical material, on the other. There is certainly nothing in Scripture itself that warrants this hard and fast distinction. To the contrary, the Bible's doctrinal, ethical, and salvific material is woven into the

mans, 1975); P. Achtemeier, *The Inspiration of Scripture* (Philadelphia: Westminster, 1980); D. Fuller, "Inspiration and Authority of the Bible," *Decision*, April, 1966; D. Fuller, "The Nature of Biblical Inerrancy," *Journal of the American Scientific Affiliation*, (June, 1972), 47–50; C. Kraft, *Christianity in Culture: A Study in Dynamic Biblical Theologizing in Cross-Cultural Perspective* (Maryknoll: Oribis, 1979).

7. To be clear, I don't *always* think the available evidence supports the historical veracity of biblical passages. Such matters must be assessed by historical-critical means and on a case-by-case basis. Yet, for reasons to be discussed in chapter 7, even if evidence forces us to conclude that a particular biblical narrative has no discernable relationship with "actual history"—that is, it is entirely fictional—I don't believe this should in any way undermine our confidence in its God-breathed nature. This would simply indicate that recounting "actual history" was apparently not among the purposes for which God inspired this particular narrative.

fabric of its historical material and vice versa. So far as I can see, the only justification for drawing a hard line between the two is that it allows scholars to create an error-free safe zone within the Bible.

I fully empathized with this concern. In the midst of the Bible's sea of human fallibilities, these folks understandably wanted to establish a domain of material that people could confidently trust to be God's authoritative, inerrant word. They were, in essence, trying to avoid the same slippery slope toward liberalism and relativism that Frank had feared I'd slide down. As sympathetic as I was, and still am, however, trying to avoid this proverbial slippery slope by carving out an inerrant safety zone within an otherwise error-filled Bible struck me as artificial and ultimately futile.

Third, I wasn't convinced that any of these proposed views were entirely consistent with the view of the Bible espoused by Jesus. Nor did they seem consistent with the way the authors of the NT or the way theologians in the premodern church tradition treated the Bible. While there have been differences of opinion on a great multitude of matters pertaining to Scripture, the bedrock assumption of theologians within the historic orthodox tradition has always been that *all* Scripture is God-breathed.

From time to time in church history, we find Christian thinkers such as Origen, who openly acknowledged that the Bible contains errors, contradictions, inaccuracies, and morally offensive material. Yet, no premodern theologian within the orthodox Christian tradition, including Origen, ever denied that the entire Bible, *including its erroneous and otherwise troubling material*, was both divinely inspired and in some sense revelatory. In this light, I eventually concluded that, whatever the way out of my conundrum might eventually look like, it wasn't going to come about by trying to quarantine the Bible's allegedly inerrant material away from its problematic material.

* * *

By the time I had completed my master's degree at YDS and entered my doctoral program at PTS in 1982, I was fairly confident of three things as it concerned Scripture. First, on the authority of Jesus, the church tradition, and my own experience, I remained convinced that all of Scripture was, in some sense, divinely inspired. I simply had not yet managed to get clear on what exactly this meant or entailed, except that I knew it couldn't possibly entail that the Bible—or some category of material within the Bible—is completely free of errors, contradictions, inaccuracies, or morally offensive material, even after all appropriate qualifications have been made.

Second, I was convinced that the historical-critical approach to Scripture was a legitimate and even necessary enterprise though, as will become clear in the following two chapters, I would soon become convinced that certain restrictions needed to be placed around how and when this method gets applied to Scripture.

On top of that, my aforementioned study of the Gospels had taught me that historical-critical scholars can come to widely divergent assessments of biblical material, owing in large part to the differing assumptions that each scholar brings to their work. Hence, my acceptance of the historical-critical method was (and is) rather cautious. And I should acknowledge that this cautiousness is reflected in the previously mentioned fact that I tend to be more persuaded by arguments defending the historicity of the biblical stories than I am by arguments against this historicity—though, as I've admitted, the latter prevails from time to time.

And third, as I've already mentioned, I was convinced that the attempt to salvage inerrancy by carving out an inerrant domain of material and quarantining it from Scripture's fallible material was artificial, implausible, and in conflict with the traditional understanding of the plenary inspiration of the Bible. Whatever else I would do with Scripture's unresolvable problems, I was convinced that they could no more be quarantined from the rest of Scripture than they could all be reasonably explained away.

* * *

Origen taught that all of the Bible's contradictions, errors, inaccuracies, and morally offensive material was divinely inspired to fulfill a higher, always Christ-centered, divine purpose. He believed that the "Holy Spirit supervised" the incorporation into the story of God, "which appeared at the first glance could neither be true or useful." But she intentionally did this "in order that . . . we should be led on to search for . . . a meaning worthy of God."[8] In Origen's view, this is one of the means by which the Spirit matures disciples.

At some point early on in my doctoral program, I began to wonder if Origen might be right. If the Bible's problems are all divinely inspired, I thought, then perhaps the only *real* problem we have with the Bible is that we tend to assume that its contradictions, errors, inaccuracies, and morally questionable material are bona fide problems. What if God inspired them to function as *assets*, not problems?

In fact, the first academic article I ever published explored the divine wisdom behind the Bible's obscure and/or confusing material.[9] Though I of course didn't know it at the time, I was already moving in the direction of the Cruciform Model of Inspiration way back in 1985! As to why it took another thirty-five years before I returned to this foundationally important topic, I can only confess that focus has never been my strong suit.

Nevertheless, I don't believe I would have ever arrived at the perspective I have today if I hadn't had the good fortune of becoming acquainted with the writings of twentieth-century theologian Karl Barth. As will become clear over the next several chapters, encountering Barth was something of a game changer for me.

8. Origen, *On First Principles*, trans. G. W. Butterworth (Gloucester, MA: Peter Smith, 1973), 4.2.9, 287. For a comprehensive of Origen's understanding of Scripture's problematic material, see G. Boyd, *Crucifixion of the Warrior God: Interpreting the Old Testaments Violent Portraits of God in Light of the Cross*, 2 vols. (Minneapolis: Fortress, 2017) 1, 417–61.

9. Though, for a variety of reasons, I centered my reflections around Pascal rather than Origen. See G. Boyd, "The Divine Wisdom of Obscurity: Pascal on the Positive Value of Scriptural Difficulties," *Journal of the Evangelical Theological Society* 28, no. 2 (1985): 195–204.

6.

Game Changer

> For Jesus, the key to understanding the Old Testament was located in his own life and work, for everything pointed to himself. —David Dockery

> [God] set it all out before us in Christ, a long-range plan in which everything would be brought together and summed up in him, everything in deepest heaven, everything on planet earth. —Ephesians 1:9 (The Message)

Shelley and I have been happily married for forty years.

Well, *mostly* happily married. We got off to a pretty rocky start.

One of the (many) difficulties we had to work through early on in our marriage revolved around how we talk about problems. I had always assumed that the only purpose for talking about a problem was to solve it as quickly as possible. There are so many other interesting and fun things you could be doing with your time; why would anyone want to spend any more time than absolutely necessary talking about problems? This seemed especially true once I entered Seminary—exactly one week after Shelley and I returned from our honeymoon—and was introduced to a vast multitude of interesting theologians and philosophers. Time spent talking about boring problems was time *not* spent reading and discussing interesting books.

So, early on in our marriage Shelley would frequently interrupt my reading to talk about a problem, and I would almost always quickly propose a solution so I could get back to reading. And, if I may set aside modesty for a moment, I'm actually pretty good at quickly and creatively solving problems. Years of practice, I guess. To my dismay, however, Shelley would usually want to keep talking about the problem, as though I hadn't just solved it! "Can we just process this a little bit more?" she would sometimes say. And I would typically respond, "What's there to process? The problem is solved!"

To my great bewilderment, Shelley seemed hurt and frustrated that I was able to solve problems so quickly. I would have thought she would have thanked me!

One time I actually proposed that we allocate two hours per week—Wednesday morning from 9:00 to 11:00 a.m.—to talk about whatever problems needed resolving while agreeing to not bring up problems (except in an emergency) outside of this time frame. (See how creatively I solved the problem of the perpetual problem-talking that had besieged our marriage?) Shelley was as dumbfounded as I imagine some of you are right now. I openly acknowledge that I was a twenty-two-year-old relational moron.

Several rather miserable months into the marriage, I was running an errand in my rusty, banged-up, 1972 Ford Pinto, which I had recently purchased from a fellow YDS student for two hundred bucks. I was listening to the only station my radio offered since its tuning knob didn't work. It happened to be locked on an AM radio talk show, and on this day the talk show host was interviewing a marriage counselor who had recently published a book, though I don't recall either the name of the counselor or book. I wasn't listening intently until I heard the interviewed counselor say: "Women tend to process problems differently than men." Instantly, I was all ears. And he continued:

> While there certainly are exceptions, men generally have one goal when discussing problems, and that is to solve them. Women, on the other hand, tend to have two goals when talking about problems. Yes, they want to *eventually* arrive at a solution, but often times their first goal is to feel like their friends or loved ones

> share their thoughts, concerns, and feelings about the problem so they can then collaborate together on how to solve it.

And then came his punch line, and it landed like a hard fist in my gut. "A husband who tries to rush to solutions without first taking the time to hear and empathize with his wife's perspective on the problem," he said, "is likely going to have a frustrated, lonely, and resentful wife."

This one remark instantly reframed everything! When it came to talking about problems, it's like I was playing checkers and Shelley was playing three-dimensional chess. Whenever a problem needed to be discussed, I was playing a *solve-as-quick-as-possible* game while Shelley was playing an *are-we-in-this-together?* game. (I would later find out she was also sometimes playing a *Do-you-love-books-more-than-me?* game.) Unless I wanted to be married to a lonely and resentful wife, I clearly needed to change my game.

I have, ever since, tried to remember to follow this maxim (which all *solve-as-quickly-as-possible* partners might want to consider adopting): *The initial goal of talking about a problem is not to solve it, but to feel united as we face this problem.* I can't tell you this is easy, because for a *solve-as-quickly-as-possible* kind of guy like me, it most definitely is *not*. Nor can I tell you I'm always successful. Shelley's had to lower her expectations about how much processing I'm actually capable of. (I thank God Shelley has some wonderful female friends whose capacity for processing problems is as amazing to me as is Shelley's). Nevertheless, this reframing of what is going on when Shelley and I talk about problems was a game changer, and I believe it's one of the reasons we've been *mostly* happily married for forty years.

* * *

I'm sure many of you have had similar experiences. You were going in one direction, but then something happened that opened your eyes and allowed you to reframe a problem, thereby launching you in a completely different direction.

Whether it's a person, idea, or event, that's what a game changer does. When it came to reconciling my belief in the plenary inspiration of Scripture with its multitude of problems, my game changer was Karl Barth.

Barth has been a game changer for multitudes of other people as well. In fact, he is almost uniformly regarded as the single most influential theologian of the twentieth century. He was also among the most prolific theologians in church history. His *magnum opus*, which is entitled, *Church Dogmatics*, is a fourteen-volume work containing over a million words! Not to mention the numerous other books and essays Barth produced in his lifetime.

I had heard about Barth and had even read portions of his *Church Dogmatics* before coming to Princeton. Most of what I heard had come from Frank and his fellow evangelical seminarians, and it was almost entirely negative (and, I would later discover, largely inaccurate). The little of Barth I had read for myself didn't resonate with me. Looking back on it, I strongly suspect that the negative preconception I had inherited of Barth from my evangelical friends so prejudiced my mind that I wasn't genuinely open to what Barth had to say.

Barth has a distinctive, intensely Christocentric way of theologizing that is so unique that readers will inevitably misunderstand him if they aren't genuinely interested in understanding Barth *on his own terms*. It's not surprising, therefore, that when I initially read Barth, I *thought* I more or less understood what he was saying, but I didn't. Nor is it surprising that Barth sounded to me like the liberal, overly subjective, overly Christocentric thinker my former evangelical friends had painted him out to be.

I was now in a very different place, however. My toiling over my conundrum from an evangelical vantage point over the previous five years had run its course, and I was now open to exploring different paradigms of thinking, not only about my conundrum, but about theology in general.

I was now in a place where I genuinely wanted to hear what the most famous theologian of the twentieth century had to say about the inspiration of Scripture.

* * *

I was working as a teaching assistant for Professor Daniel Migliore, who, like so many other faculty at PTS at the time, had been heavily influenced by Barth. Both in class and in personal conversations, Migliore frequently referred to Barth's perspective on whatever issue happened to be under discussion. And given my respect for Migliore, this led me to suspect that I had perhaps dismissed Barth too quickly.

After one particular class that touched on the inspiration of Scripture, I asked Migliore about Barth's understanding of biblical inspiration. Migliore offered a two- or three-minute summary, which I found more puzzling than enlightening. Noticing my bewilderment, Migliore said to me, "I think it's one of those things you need to read and digest on your own to truly understand." He then directed me to the volume and approximate page numbers of *Church Dogmatics* that contained Barth's reflections on biblical inspiration.[1]

Not since my initial reading of C. S. Lewis had a thinker rocked my world like Barth did. While I think there are significant problems and caveats in Barth's perspective, as will become clear in the following two chapters, and while the Cruciform Model of Inspiration that I'll be advocating modifies and supplements his perspective in several significant ways, Barth's reflections opened my eyes to a way out of my conundrum and helped shape the basic perspective on Scripture I've held ever since.

Throughout the remainder of this chapter I will spell out what I consider to be the most important foundational aspects of Barth's understanding of biblical inspiration.

* * *

To begin, while each of the perspectives we've reviewed thus far have been based on the traditional assumption that Scripture is itself the Word of God, Barth draws a clear distinction *between*

1. Karl Barth, *Church Dogmatics* I/2, *The Doctrine of the Word of God*, trans. G. T. Thomson and H. Knight (Edinburgh: T & T Clark, 1956), 457–537. All bracket references to page numbers in the text over the next four chapters are to this work.

Scripture and the Word of God. According to Barth, God's one and only Word is Jesus Christ (512–13). This singular revelation contains within itself a disclosure of the entire triune God, for Jesus reveals the transcendent Father, and we are empowered to recognize and receive this revelation by faith through the power of God's indwelling Spirit (483).

For Barth, therefore, Scripture is breathed by God not to function as a revelation *in its own right*, but to rather serve as a *witness to* the one revelation of the triune God in Jesus Christ (463). Yet, perhaps the most distinctive aspect of Barth's understanding of biblical inspiration is that he believes Scripture becomes a divinely inspired witness to the Word of God only when God sovereignly decides for it to do so. When this happens, but only when this happens, Scripture *can*, in a secondary and derivative sense, be identified as "God's Word" (514, 527).

According to Barth, therefore, we need to understand Scripture in two very distinct ways. We must first consider what the biblical writings are *in and of themselves*. Then we must understand what these writings *become* when God freely chooses to make the Word present in Scripture and when God awakens people's faith to discern this Word—which is to say, when God sovereignly causes Scripture to function as "God's Word."

* * *

Considered in and of itself, the Bible is an ordinary, fallible, collection of ancient human writings, according to Barth (507). "At every point," he says, the Bible "is the vulnerable word of man" (512). As such, biblical writings can and should be evaluated by the historical-critical method, just as we would evaluate any other ancient writings (507).

When evaluated in this fashion, according to Barth, we discover that biblical authors had the same "capacity to err" as well as the same capacity to be "sinful in their actions" that all humans have, even as they wrote their divinely inspired works (510, 529).[2] Moreover, we find that biblical authors were as

2. Barth sometimes insists that we should restrict ourselves to speaking only of *the*

conditioned by the assumptions of their surrounding culture as are other ancient authors (508). Indeed, Barth contends that much of the material in the OT so closely parallels the writings of Israel's ANE neighbors that it is sometimes "impossible to distinguish between them" (509).

Barth further argues that the capacity of biblical authors to be influenced by their surrounding culture and to err applies not only to the Bible's "philosophical, historical and ethical content," but even to its "religious and theological" material (507; cf. 495). Barth goes so far as to claim that, when assessed the way we assess other ancient works, we can discern no qualitative difference between the writings that comprise Scripture and all other human writings. Moreover, Barth claims that we must accept that "we can make little or nothing of large tracts of the Bible, as is often the case with the records of other men" (507). And this too is as true of the Bible's "religious and theological material as it is of everything else we find in the Bible" (507).

Precisely because the writings of Scripture are as culturally conditioned and as prone to err and sin as other human writings, Barth acknowledges that it is possible for contemporary readers to "take offence at the Bible." In fact, apart from "the miracle of faith," which is brought about by God's free grace alone, Barth believes "we are bound to take offence at it" (507). Among other things, the culturally conditioned perspectives of biblical authors frequently clashes with our own culturally conditioned perspectives. For example, while modern people place a premium on the distinction between history, on the one hand, and "saga and legend," on the other, Barth contends that biblical authors "know nothing of this distinction" (509).[3]

In short, Barth contends that biblical writings should be critically evaluated the same way we critically evaluate all other ancient works. And when we do this, Barth contends that we

capacity of biblical authors to err and refrain from alleging that they ever *actually* err (508–9). At other times, however, he claims that these authors are "capable and *actually guilty* of error in their spoken and written word" (529, emphasis added). It is unclear to me how these two statements can be reconciled.

3. I believe Barth is guilty of overstatement here. NT authors are particularly interested in distinguishing their Gospel from "saga and legend." For a discussion, see Eddy and Boyd, *Jesus Legend*.

find nothing in them that distinguishes them from other writings of their time and place in history.

* * *

At the same time, as I noted above, Barth holds that this ordinary collection of fallible human writings comes to bear witness to Jesus Christ, the one and only Word of God, when God freely chooses to have the eternal Word dwell in these human writings and when God freely chooses to have the Spirit bring about "the miracle of faith" that allows people to receive and submit to this Word (507). "The miracle which has to take place if the Bible is to rise up and speak to us as the Word of God," Barth writes, "has to always consist in an awakening and strengthening of our faith" (512).

Barth claims that the choice to embrace faith is a "free human decision" (512). At the same time, Barth was a Calvinist who held that human free will is compatible with God's sovereign control over all things, including our free decisions. Barth thus describes the decision to embrace faith both as a "free human decision" and as a "free decision of God." And, of course, in the Calvinist view, it is only God's free decision that makes the free human decision possible (513). If God hadn't decided to give us faith, in other words, we never would have chosen it on our own.

Inspiration clearly isn't a static attribute of Scripture, according to Barth. Rather, the inspiration of Scripture is a dynamic event that "God Himself decides and wills and does in divine freedom and superiority and power" (503). It is, in short, "a miracle of the divine Majesty in its condescension and mercy" (513).

* * *

This miraculous event doesn't in any way diminish any of Scripture's fallible human qualities, any more than Jesus's divinity diminishes any aspect of his fallible humanity (528). However, while the means by which this miraculous event takes place is an "inaccessible mystery" (504), God's gracious choice to have the biblical writings bear witness to Jesus Christ completely transforms every aspect of the canonical writings.

For Barth, Paul's teaching in 2 Timothy 3:16, which affirms that all Scripture is God-breathed, implies that "we have to hear all [the] words" of biblical authors "with the same measure of respect." So too, Barth argues that "it would be arbitrary to relate their inspiration only to such parts of their witness as perhaps appear important to us" (517–18). Even the most "debatable and least assimilable parts" of Scripture can be used by God to bear witness to the Word of God, Jesus Christ (719).

It's apparent, then, that when God inspires the Bible to function as a witness to God's Word, even the most problematic aspects of the Bible function in this manner. So, while Barth distinguishes between the Bible considered in and of itself and the Bible considered as an inspired witness to the Word, he has no place for the sorts of distinctions qualified inerrantists make, as we saw in the previous chapter. *Everything* in Scripture, from its errors and contradictions to its morally offensive depictions of God to its most sublime and insightful material is equally inspired by God when God sovereignly chooses to have it bear witness to Jesus Christ.

I finally had found a contemporary theologian who unambiguously affirmed the plenary inspiration of the Bible while nevertheless boldly embracing all of its problems. While the Bible shares all the qualities that are common to all other human writings, according to Barth, it is transformed into a book that is as unique as the incarnate Word himself once God causes the Word to dwell in these human writings, for the Bible now *participates in* this utterly unique incarnate Word of God (463). Indeed, in keeping with a long tradition within the church, Barth argues that the manner in which Scripture is fully divine and fully human when God causes the Word to be present in Scripture is analogous to the manner in which Jesus is both fully God and fully human (501, 512–13).

* * *

As much as Barth emphasizes the need for God to breathe through Scripture in the present for it to serve as a witness to

Jesus Christ, this is not an *ad hoc* decision on God's part, as though biblical authors composed their writings on their own and God then simply decided to appropriate them as witnesses. To the contrary, Barth affirms the church's traditional view that biblical authors wrote their canonical material under the inspiring influence of the Holy Spirit (517). In fact, though most commentators seem to miss this, Barth even affirms the "verbal inspiration" of the entire canon of Scripture (518). Sounding at times like a conservative evangelical, Barth insists that "the Holy Spirit" is "the real author of what is stated or written in Scripture" (505).

Yet, while Barth affirms "verbal inspiration," it's important to note that this "does not mean that God's revelation is now before us in any kind of divine revealedness," or that divine inspiration is an abiding quality of Scripture that is "perspicuous to everybody" (517; cf. 502). To the contrary, as we saw above, there are no objective qualities of the Bible that distinguish it from other human writings, according to Barth. When people understand inspiration to be an abiding quality of Scripture that is "perspicuous to everybody" rather than as a dynamic event that can only be seen with the eyes of faith, Barth contends they are reducing the Bible to a magical "book of oracles" and "an instrument of direct impartation" (507). In Barth's view, it violates "the sovereignty and freedom of God" (513) to think that inspiration is a discernable abiding quality of Scripture. And, he continues:

> God is not an attribute of something else, even if this something else is the Bible. . . . He is Lord even over the Bible and in the Bible. The statement that the Bible is the Word of God cannot therefore say that the Word of God is tied to the Bible. On the contrary, what it must say is that the Bible is tied to the Word of God (513).

Along the same lines, Barth insists that it is vitally important we remember that, when we confess the Bible to be "the Word of God," we are claiming that the Bible is "the Word *of God*." Which means that our confession that the Bible is "the Word of God" isn't actually about the Bible itself; it's rather a confession about "a free decision of God" that is completely outside of "human control and foresight" (513, 527).

In this light, Barth argues that our confession that God inspired all the words of Scripture is actually a confession about "the relationship between God and Scripture," and this "can be understood only as a disposing act and decision of God Himself" (504). The initial inspiration of the biblical writings, in other words, must be understood only as the first "phase" that the Word passes through in the process of coming to us (517). This phase functions as a sort of promissory note regarding God's future free decision to use these words as witnesses to God's Word. But as we've seen, these words only become revelatory, and inspired in the full sense of the word, when God chooses to act on this promise by activating our faith, thereby allowing us to miraculously encounter the divine Word in these human words.

In Barth's view, therefore, when we confess the Bible to be the Word of God, we are by faith remembering how God has miraculously used this fallible collection of writings as a witness to the Word in the past, and we are by faith trusting that God will continue to use them in this fashion in the present and future (502). But we can only pray that this miracle will continue to take place, according to Barth (514). For, while our reading of Scripture may be under our control, we can never control the "free decision of God" that miraculously transforms Scripture into God's inspired witness to the living Word.

* * *

One final aspect of Barth's theology of Scripture needs to be noted. While Barth embraces the historical-critical approach to Scripture when considering the Bible in and of itself, he also saw that it had limited applicability when reading or hearing the Bible preached as the word of God. For the goal of reading Scripture as God's Word is not to interrogate Scripture, as the historical-critical method requires, but to rather allow the Word to interrogate us and shape us through Scripture. "I have read many books," Barth once said, "but the Bible reads me."[4]

According to Barth as well as an increasing chorus of biblical scholars and theologians, while it is legitimate to apply historical-critical methods to the Bible, if we hope to read or hear it as a witness to Jesus Christ the way God intended, we must read or hear it in a *pre-critical** fashion, along the lines of the way the early church read and heard Scripture.[5] Our concern when reading Scripture this way can't be to get behind the text to discern the pre-canonical history of different sources that were used to compile the text. Nor can our concern be to get behind the text to discern the degree to which it is or is not anchored in "actual history." These concerns are perfectly appropriate for a historical-critical study of Scripture, but they are distractions and hinderances when reading or hearing Scripture to encounter Jesus. In the words of Hans Frei, these historical-critical concerns "eclipse" the power of the biblical narrative.[6]

When we read or hear Scripture with faith that it is the God-breathed witness to the Word, according to Barth, we are miraculously "led by Bible 'history' far out beyond what is elsewhere called history—into a new world, into the world of God."[7] And once we've, by faith, entered this new world, Barth held that everything in Scripture "should be taken literally; not in a shallow but a deep sense."[8]

The "shallow" sense of *literal* is the one that the historical-critical approach attempts to discern: To what degree is this biblical story literally—that is, *historically*—true? The "deep"

4. Quoted in B, Hull, *The Complete Book of Discipleship* (Colorado Springs, CO: NavPress, 2006), 218.

5. This precritical way of reading Scripture is one aspect of what is commonly referred to as "The Theological Interpretation of the Bible" (TIS). For an excellent introduction, see D. J. Treier, *Introducing Theology Interpretation of Scripture: Recovering a Christian Practice* (Grand Rapids: Baker Academic, 2008).

6. H. Frei, *The Eclipse of the Biblical Narrative: A Study in Eighteenth and Nineteenth Century Hermeneutics* (New Haven, CT: Yale University Press, 1974).

7. K. Barth, "The Strange New World Within the Bible," in *The Word of God and the Word of Man*, trans. D. Horton (Gloucester, MA: Peter Smith, 1978), 37.

8. K. Barth, *Church Dogmatics* III/1, *The Doctrine of Creation*, Part I, ed. G. W. Bromiley and T. T. Torrance, trans. G. W. Bromiley (London: T&T Clark, 2009), 94.

sense of *literal*, by contrast, concerns the significance that each character and event within the biblical narrative takes on when we, by faith, enter the world of this story, trusting that these characters and events bear witness to Jesus Christ.

This distinction is often expressed in academic theological circles by the German words *geschichte* and *historish*. *Geschichte* refers to stories about the past whose significance has nothing to do with whether or not they are grounded in "actual history." By contrast, *historish* refers to "actual history," insofar as this can be reconstructed by historical-critical means. According to Barth, when reading or hearing Scripture as a witness to the Word, we must read it as *geschichte* and without any concern about the degree to which it may also constitute *historish*.

* * *

Such is the broad outline of Barth's distinctive reflections on biblical inspiration. In the following two chapters, I will finish setting the stage for our discussion of the Cruciform Model of Inspiration in part 2 by first reviewing four aspects of Barth's theology of Scripture that I find compelling and that contributed to him exercising a game-changing influence on my thoughts on biblical inspiration, and then by raising three sets of criticism against Barth's perspective.

7.

Foundational Insights

> Jesus is the one mediator between God and man. He is thus the hermeneutic principle for every word from God. Thus the prime question to put to every text is about how it testifies to Jesus. —Graeme Goldsworthy

> All things have been handed over to me by my Father; and no one knows the Son except the Father, and no one knows the Father except the Son and anyone to whom the Son chooses to reveal him. —Matthew 11:27

I've come to believe that a person's mental conception of God is the single most important fact about their life. The beauty of our relationship with God can never outrun the beauty of our mental conception of God, which is why I believe it's so vitally important that we base everything we think about God on Jesus Christ.

It was Karl Barth who first taught me this.

In this chapter, I will discuss Barth's intensely Christocentric focus as well as three other aspects of his thought that have influenced my thinking on the inspiration of Scripture.

* * *

To begin, Barth convinced me that Jesus is the one and only Word of God and that all Scripture is inspired for the ultimate purpose of bearing witness to him. As we have already seen, according to John, Jesus himself reflected this perspective when he taught that "the scriptures . . . testify on my behalf" and that Moses "wrote about me."[1] Indeed, he claimed that he was the "life" that Scripture was inspired to lead people to.[2]

Similarly, Luke recounts how, soon after rising from the dead, Jesus helped two discouraged disciples see that "all the scriptures" were about him, and, more specifically, about why it was "necessary that the Messiah should suffer before entering into his glory."[3] A short while later, Luke says, Jesus opened the minds of other disciples to "understand the scriptures," thereby enabling them to see that "the law of Moses, the prophets, and the psalms"—in short, all Scripture—were about him, and, more specifically, about his sacrificial death and resurrection.[4]

Paul similarly taught that Jesus died and rose from the dead "in accordance with the scriptures."[5] As N. T. Wright has argued, Paul isn't merely claiming that there are a few passages that explicitly predict Jesus's death and resurrection. He is rather claiming that the entire OT points toward, and finds its fulfillment in, Jesus's death and resurrection.[6] As Paul says elsewhere, everything God has ever promised finds its fulfillment in Christ.[7] Understanding *how* all Scripture bears witness to Jesus, and especially to his death and resurrection, will play an important role in the Cruciform Model. For now, however, it is enough to simply grasp Barth's insight that Jesus is, in fact, the Word to which all the words of Scripture point.

We find this Christocentric understanding of Scripture reflected throughout the NT.[8] Consider, for example, how the author of Hebrews opens his letter:

1. John 5:39, 46.
2. John 5:40.
3. Luke 24:25–7.
4. Luke 24:44–5.
5. 1 Cor 15:3–4.
6. N. T. Wright, *The Day the Revolution Began: Reconsidering the Meaning of Jesus's Crucifixion* (New York: HarperCollins, 2016), 280–81.
7. 2 Cor 1:20.
8. For a much more comprehensive review of the NT material that supports seeing Jesus as the absolute centerpiece of Scripture, see G. Boyd, *Crucifixion of the Warrior God: Interpreting Scripture's Violent Depictions of God in Light of the Cross*, 2 vols. (Minneapolis: Fortress, 2017) 1:35–140.

> In the past God spoke to our ancestors through the prophets at many times and in various ways, but in these last days he has spoken to us by his Son, whom he appointed heir of all things, and through whom also he made the universe. The Son is the radiance of God's glory and the exact representation of his being.[9]

This author is here contrasting the revelation of God in Jesus with the revelations that people in the OT received. While previous revelations were mediated through prophets, he says, in this final epoch of history—in "these last days"—God has revealed Godself through the "Son," which is simply this author's way of referring to God incarnate.[10] The author of Hebrews is thus claiming that, whereas God's Word or self-revelation was mediated through *others* in the past, Jesus is God revealing Godself *in person.*

Moreover, this author says previous revelations came in "various ways." The Greek word for this is *polymerōs*, and it can be translated as "diverse portions" (ASV) or even as "glimpses of truth" (J. B. Phillips). By contrast, Jesus is the very "radiance of God's glory." When God displays God's glory, the author of Hebrews is saying, it looks like Jesus. Which means, insofar as people in OT times caught "glimpses of truth," they were seeing the same Word that we see in Jesus. They just couldn't see him as clearly as we can, now that he's personally revealed himself.

Finally, whereas the "glimpses of truth" that people received in the OT gave them approximations of what God is like, the Son is "the exact representation of God's being" or essence (*hupostasis*). The author is thus saying that *Jesus reveals exactly what God is like all the way down to God's very essence.*

This passage confirms Barth's contention that Jesus isn't merely one revelation of God alongside others in the Bible, or even merely the best revelation among other revelations in the Bible. Jesus, rather, is the one and only revelation or Word of God. Hence, insofar as God has revealed Godself to anyone, at any time, and to any degree, they were encountering the one

9. Heb 1:1–3.

10. See Heb 1:6, 8, 10. See R. Bauckham, "The Divinity of Jesus in the Letter of Hebrews," in *Jesus and the God of Israel: God Crucified and Other Studies on the New Testament's Christology of Divine Identity* (Grand Rapids: Eerdmans, 2008), 233–53.

Word of God that was made flesh in Jesus Christ.[11] It's just that, prior to the Word becoming flesh, people only caught glimpses of this Word. I thus believe Barth reflects the perspective of the NT when he contends that we must read all Scripture through the lens of Jesus and with the understanding that all Scripture, when properly interpreted, bears witness to Jesus.

* * *

A second aspect of Barth's thought that I find invaluable concerns his understanding of the unique posture people should assume when encountering Scripture as God's Word. Like Barth, I'm convinced that, whereas the historical-critical approach is always trying to get at the historical reality *behind* the text, our goal when encountering Scripture as God's inspired story is to enter into *the world of the text itself*, exercising faith that God will encounter us there as God uses this text to bear witness to the living Word.

On this note, it's important to remember that neither Jesus nor the early church read Scripture with the goal of answering the kind of questions that the historical-critical method is designed to ask and answer. As I noted in the previous chapter, they read and interpreted the Bible in a pre-critical fashion, which, I submit, is sufficient warrant for us to do the same. Moreover, when Jesus quoted the OT or alluded to biblical characters or events, he was endorsing *the text* of Scripture. He wasn't pre-endorsing answers to contemporary historical-critical questions concerning how various biblical characters or events where composed or the degree to which these characters or events correspond with "actual history."

We might say that Jesus endorsed Scripture as divinely inspired *geschichte*, not *historish*, and the same could be said for the authors of the NT. And since I have reason to think Jesus was not mistaken in endorsing Scripture as *geschichte*, I feel compelled to trust that the text of Scripture is completely God-breathed, regardless of how well it does or does not correspond

11. In chapters 13 and 14 I will address the question of how we are to make sense of the OT's sub-Christ-like portraits of God.

to "actual history."[12] As Douglas Earl has pointedly stated the matter, "it is *the text* that the church has accepted as authoritative and *not* the history behind the text."[13]

This also applies to the problem of Jesus's references to Moses as the author of the Pentateuch. Jesus was not pre-endorsing the "right" answer to the historical-critical question of how the Pentateuch was formed. As I argued in the previous chapter, Jesus was simply reflecting the conventional first-century association of Moses with the Pentateuch. The historical-critical debate over the various sources that comprise the Pentateuch would have been as far from Jesus's mind as the nagging contemporary question of how to reconcile general relativity theory with quantum theory.[14]

* * *

A third important aspect of Barth's thought that has strongly influenced me, and which pertains directly to the thesis of this book, concerns his understanding of the Bible's inspired imperfections. As we saw in the previous chapter, Barth holds that even the "most debatable and least assimilable" aspects of Scripture are God-breathed for the purpose of bearing witness to Christ (719).

It's not that this material can be shown to be divinely inspired once an apologist puts the best possible spin on it to render it less offensive and more digestible. Rather, according to Barth, the very offensive and indigestible nature of some of the Bible's problematic material must be considered just as divinely inspired as the most beautiful and obviously insightful biblical material. Other than Origen, I know of no other theologian in church history who so clearly espoused this perspective.

In direct opposition to those evangelicals who assume that a perfect God must breath a perfect book, Barth argued that

12. For my reasoning behind accepting the NT as divinely inspired, see chapter 3.

13. D. S. Earl, *The Joshua Delusion? Rethinking Genocide in the Bible* (Eugene, OR: Cascade Books. 2010), 5 (first emphasis added, second emphasis original).

14. Something similar could be argued for Paul's references to Adam in Romans 5:12–21. See P. Enns, *The Evolution of Adam: What the Bible Does and Doesn't Say About Human Origins* (Grand Rapids: Brazos, 2012).

we only understand what it means to confess the Bible to be God's Word "when we recognize its human imperfection in face of its divine perfection, and its divine perfection in spite of its human imperfection" (508). Barth is claiming that the Bible's imperfections, including its offensive and difficult-to-digest material, magnify God's perfection by demonstrating that, in God's sovereign freedom, God is able and willing to display God's greatness by using "low and despised [things] of the world," as Paul taught.[15] The fact that God is able to breathe God's Word through such material highlights all the more the "miracle of the divine Majesty in its condescension and mercy" (513).

In my estimation, Barth is simply applying to the Bible Paul's teaching that God's power "is made perfect in . . . weakness."[16]

* * *

Fourth, and finally, while Barth resists saying Scripture is in any sense "infallible" (e.g., 528), his writings actually helped me understand how I could, and why I should, affirm this of Scripture. I will now argue that the logic of Barth's position points in this direction, for in his view, when God sovereignly decides to miraculously use these authors to bear witness to the Word, it cannot fail to happen. Which is to say, it happens *infallibly*.

Consider that, according to Barth, *whenever* God miraculously causes the Word to be present in the words of Scripture, it is *always* accompanied by God miraculously giving people the gift of faith through the power of the Spirit to discern the Word dwelling in these human words. Indeed, as Barth construes the matter, these are two sides of the same revelatory event. Within Barth's framework, therefore, it would impossible for people to have faith in the Bible as God's Word and *not* discern the Word abiding in these words. As such, it seems appropriate to say that, for Barth, the fallible writings of the Bible infallibly bear witness to Jesus Christ when God freely decides to have them do so.

15. 1 Cor 1:18–30.
16. 2 Cor 12:9.

By recognizing that the confession that the Bible is the inspired word of God is a confession about "the relationship between God and Scripture" instead of about the Bible itself, Barth had shown me a potential way out of the conundrum I'd been wrestling with for six years. I now had a paradigm that enabled me to trust the Bible to infallibly accomplish all that God intends it to accomplish without needing to deny or to feel embarrassed by the fallibility of the biblical writings themselves.

* * *

Now, as we saw in the previous chapter, Barth speaks about this infallible revelatory event as being simultaneously a "free decision of man" and a "free decision of God" (513). Indeed, throughout *Church Dogmatics* Barth reflects the Calvinistic assumption that there is no incompatibility between saying God determined our actions, on the one hand, and saying we freely chose our actions, on the other.

For example, Barth at one point says, "The sovereignty of God and of God's good-pleasure consists in the fact that it is a sovereignty which orders history, the content of God's eternal will." This sovereignty is mysterious, however, for it "must be thought of as the mystery of the human decision as well as the divine." Yet, Barth immediately goes on to a reject any sort of "*synergism*,"* arguing that "there can be no co-operation or reciprocal action of any kind between any such mystery in man and the mystery of the predestining God."[17]

It would obviously take us far off track were I to attempt to enter into the determinism verses free will debate. For our present purposes it must suffice for me to register my deep reservations about the biblical basis, and even the basic intelligibility, of this *compatiblistic conception of human freedom*.*[18] My only point in even bringing this issue up is that one could argue that the infallible way God uses biblical authors to bear

17. K. Barth, *Church Dogmatics* II/2, *The Doctrine of God*, trans. G. W. Bromiley, et al. (Edinburgh: T & T Clark, 1957), 193–94.

18. For my critique of divine determinism, see G. Boyd, "God Limits His Control," in *Four Views on Divine Providence*, ed. D. Jowers (Grand Rapids: Zondervan, 2011), 183–208.

witness to Jesus in Barth's thought presupposes this compatiblistic conception of freedom. As such, one could argue that the Barthian conception of biblical infallibility could not be utilized by an *Arminian** such as myself, for Arminians believe that divine determinism and free will are incompatible with each other.[19]

This objection can be quickly answered simply by distinguishing between God's free decision to use the Bible as an infallible witness to Jesus, on the one hand, and the human free decision to trust the Bible to function as an infallible witness, on the other.

As an Arminian, I can agree with Barth that the Bible is an infallible witness to Jesus when God decides to use it in this fashion *and* when people freely choose to trust Scripture for this purpose. I have to get off the Barthian train, however, when he claims that God's decision to cause God's Word to dwell in the words of Scripture is *always*, by God's sovereign will, accompanied by a human decision to affirm Scripture as the inspired story of God. I rather think humans always have the ability to grieve the heart of God by resisting God's Spirit, thereby rejecting God's good purposes for themselves.[20] I can therefore affirm with Barth that the Bible will infallibly accomplish all that God intends it to accomplish when people freely choose to trust it for this purpose. I would simply add that people remain free to *not* trust the Bible for this purpose, if they so choose.

* * *

The four aspects of Barth's theology of Scripture that I've just outlined go a long way toward expressing the game-changing

19. I am best known as "an open theist" rather than an "Arminian," but I consider open theism to be a subdivision of Arminianism. I identify as Arminian in this context because the point of this objection applies to all Arminians, whether they hold to the traditional view of the future as exhaustively settled and known by God as such, or whether they hold that the future is partly comprised of possibilities and known by God as such, as I and other open theists believe. For the debate between classical Arminians and the open view of the future, see J. Beilby and P. Eddy, eds., *Divine Foreknowledge: Four Views* (Downers Grove, IL: InterVarsity, 2001).

20. See e.g., Isa 63:10; Luke 7:31; Acts 7:51; Eph 4:30; Heb 3:8, 15; 4:7.

way Barth impacted my thinking on Scripture. But even our greatest heroes have fallibilities. Over time, I've come to discern a number of problems and shortcomings in Barth's perspective, and wrestling with these has also helped move me in the direction of the Cruciform Model of Inspiration. Consequently, I can think of no better way to finishing setting the stage for my discussion of this model of inspiration than to review some of these shortcomings.

8.

Critiquing Barth

> What can be asserted without evidence can also be dismissed without evidence. —Christopher Hitchens

> After his suffering he presented himself alive to them by many convincing proofs, appearing to them during forty days and speaking about the kingdom of God. —Acts 1:3

I had been a Christian for almost a year when two guys wearing white shirts and ties showed up at my door. Yes, they were Mormons. Given my recent conversion, I was eager to talk theology with anyone who was willing, so I invited them in for a chat. They were very pleasant gentlemen, and after they presented their little spiel, they let me present mine, which, as you suspected, is the only reason I'd invited them in to begin with. Sadly, they did not convert.

Instead, just as they were about to leave, one of the gentlemen told me that it was written in the Book of Mormon that if anyone read this book with a sincere heart, God would reveal to them that this book was truly divinely inspired. He told me that this was how he became a Mormon. I asked him what that experience was like, to which he replied with a wry smile, "Just read it: you'll see." I'm not sure if it was because this man was so obviously sincere or because I was just intrigued by this different religious text, but I actually started reading this book.

And even though I was skeptical, I tried to remain open to the possibility that God might somehow reveal to me that this book was inspired.

It didn't happen.

Okay, I didn't read the *whole* thing. Frankly, I found it pretty boring and hard to follow. But I read about half of it—okay, maybe closer to a third—which I figured was enough to give God the opportunity to tell me this book was divinely inspired, if in fact it was. But it left me wondering: What did this Mormon guy experience when he read this book that convinced him it was from God?

What troubled me most was that, like this Mormon fellow, I based my faith largely on the dramatic experiences of God I talked about in the introduction to this book. I didn't know if this guy's "revelation" about the Book of Mormon was dramatic, but it obviously was enough to win his allegiance. And, on top of this, the one conversation I had with these two gentlemen sufficed to make it clear that our different belief systems were incompatible at a number of points, which meant that we both couldn't be right in thinking our experience confirmed the truth of our beliefs.

This was when I first began to toil over how much credibility I should give to my own spiritual experiences. If this guy was mistaken, despite having an experience that was powerful enough to convince him the Book of Mormon was true, then I had to admit the possibility that I might be mistaken, my dramatic experiences of God notwithstanding. Which meant that, when it comes to determining the truth of any belief system, or any religious book, we have to appeal to considerations other than people's subjective experiences.

Following my engagement with these Mormons, I actually began to investigate their claim that the Book of Mormon is divinely inspired, and I had just begun to find some pretty compelling refuting evidence when I decided I needed to set this research project aside because I had more pressing issues. You see, I was beginning classes at the University of Minnesota in a couple weeks, and I had just registered for a class entitled Introduction to Evolutionary Biology. I had three whole books

I needed to read if I was going to refute this godless professor and save this class!

I mention my encounter with these Mormons because it highlights one of the most fundamental problems I have with Barth's theology. Barth is a fideist, which means he thinks the Christian faith is self-authenticating. In this chapter I will first critique Barth's fideism and then turn my attention to his dynamic concept of inspiration, which is closely connected to it.

* * *

According to Barth, the Bible's inspiration is "a miracle which we cannot explain apart from faith, or rather apart from the Word of God in which faith believes" (506). Nor can we provide any "reasons" or "justification for our attitude" toward Scripture (461). In fact, Barth argued that it "is important to be on our guard against the view that we have to prove or justify this position" (460). Our faith rather presupposes that "the Bible has already proved itself to be the Word of God" (506).

While this way of thinking is prevalent in the Reformed tradition that Barth was steeped in, I confess I have never understood its appeal. Barth is essentially arguing that the only proof that the Bible is the inspired story of God that believers need is the fact that they believe the Bible is the inspired story of God. This sounds to me no different from someone saying, "The proof that I believe the right thing is that I *believe* I believe the right thing." Not the strongest argument in the world. It seems to me that rational people ought to be able to provide reasons why they believe what they believe, as opposed to all the other possible things they could believe. And these reasons should not simply be restatements of the belief itself.

Now, I could find a modicum of plausibility to this way of thinking if Barth associated the "miracle of faith" with some sort of self-authenticating experience, such as I and my Mormon friend had done. This wouldn't make Barth's fideism more compelling, in my opinion, since it would still leave us with no way of determining whose alleged self-authenticating experience is genuine. But associating the "miracle of faith" with a dramatic religious experience would at least make Barth's position more intelligible. We can at least understand people deciding to believe in something on the grounds of a religious experience they've had, even if we deem this experience an inadequate basis for drawing such a conclusion.

Unfortunately, while Barth grants that some people may sometimes have a religious experience of some sort when they read or hear the Bible, he explicitly *denies* that these sorts of experiences should serve as evidence that the Bible is actually the divinely inspired story of God (460–61, 506). The only proof, Barth repeatedly insists, is the miracle of faith itself. And that, I submit, is a position that comes close to being unintelligible. As I said, its tantamount to claiming that the proof that what I believe is true is that I believe that what I believe is true. I, for one, have no idea what Barth means by "proof" when he uses it in this fashion.

Not only this, but, if Christians accept that the "miracle" of our faith in the Bible as the story of God is all that is needed to prove that the Bible is in fact the inspired story of God, how could we possibly object when Mormons or Muslims or any other faith group justifies their faith in their revered holy books or their particular belief systems by employing this same circular reasoning? Unless we can give reasons as to *why* we choose to believe in the Bible rather than the Book of Mormon or the Quran or any other alleged divinely inspired book, there literally is *no reason* people should listen to our appeal to believe in the Bible rather than any of these other books.

Barth's fideism is also inconsistent with what Scripture itself has to say about proof. For example, Luke tells us that Jesus provided his disciples with "many convincing proofs" that he had in fact risen from the dead.[1] He didn't expect people to believe he rose from the dead without sufficient reason to do so. Similarly, while the risen Jesus commends all who believe in him without having seen him, according to John, he nevertheless provided the doubting Thomas with the proof he needed by inviting him to touch the wounds in his hands and side that remained from his crucifixion.[2]

1. Acts 1:3.
2. John 20:26–28.

This fits a pattern we find throughout Scripture. God consistently invites people to use their brains to discern truth. When Abraham called Yahweh out on the carpet for planning on having Sodom and Gomorrah destroyed, God didn't shut him down; God patiently reasoned with him.[3] And, most significantly, in response to a question about which was the greatest commandment, Jesus replied, "You shall love the Lord your God with all your heart, and with all your soul, and with *all your mind*"—and minds, we should note, are made for *thinking*.[4]

Yes, faith always goes beyond what reason can prove, and this is as true in principle when you have faith that the airplane you're boarding will not crash as when you decide to make Jesus Lord over your life. But faith need not, and should not, ever be divorced from, let alone go against, reason.

* * *

The second set of criticisms I'd like to raise concerns Barth's dynamic conception of the Bible's inspiration. To avoid any misunderstanding, however, I would first like to state my agreement with Barth on three fundamental matters.

First, I grant Barth's claim that the Bible's inspiration isn't "perspicuous to everybody" (517). While I believe there are compelling reasons to accept the Bible's divine inspiration, its God-breathed nature is far from obvious to the natural mind. Indeed, I concur with Barth that, when read without faith, the Bible appears to be little more than an ordinary collection of ancient, fallible, human writings.

I further grant Barth's contention that the Bible only becomes *revelatory* to a person when they yield to the Spirit and decide to accept the Bible as God's divinely inspired witness to the Word. To the nonbeliever, the Bible may reveal a great deal about the religious, ethical, and social perspectives of ancient Israelites and early Christians. But, since Jesus is the one Word or revelation of God, as we discussed in the previous chapter,

3. Gen 18:18–33.

4. Matt 22:37 (emphasis added).

if people don't encounter Jesus in Scripture, the Bible can't be considered revelatory to them.

And, finally, I grant Barth's claim that the living Word of God can't be bound to the Bible that bears witness to him. Among other things, as the second Person of the Trinity, the living Word is perpetually at work throughout the world to bring as much light to people as they are capable of receiving.[5] Moreover, the living Word is *a Person*, and when someone places their faith in this person, they enter into a saving personal relationship with the triune God that goes beyond anything that propositions could ever accomplish or fully convey.

Having granted this much, however, there are six objections that I feel need to be raised against Barth's dynamic conception of inspiration. First, I'm bewildered as to how Barth can affirm the "verbal inspiration" of Scripture and yet insist that divine inspiration isn't an abiding quality of Scripture. If God inspired just these words to be in Scripture, as Barth claims, how can this fact not be an abiding attribute of these words?

As I said a moment ago, I grant that these words only become *revelatory* when a person yields to the Spirit and chooses to read the Bible as the God-breathed story of God. But I see no reason to grant Barth's view that this entails that the Bible isn't fully divinely inspired until a person decides to believe it is so. When it comes to the inspiration of Scripture, Barth seems to have collapsed the distinction between *objective reality* and the *subjective experience* of objective reality. Just because only people of faith acknowledge the Bible's inspiration doesn't mean the Bible is only inspired when people have faith in it.

Second, it seems to me that the way Barth actually treats Scripture throughout his *Church Dogmatics*, and other theological writings, presupposes that inspiration is an abiding quality of Scripture. For example, as we saw in the previous chapter, when discussing the God-breathed nature of biblical authors, Barth argues that, "it would be arbitrary to relate their inspiration only to such parts of their witness as perhaps appear important to us, or not to their words as such but only to the views and thoughts which evoke them." For this reason, Barth

5. John 1: 9; Acts 17:26–27.

contends, "we have to hear all [biblical author's] words with the same measure of respect" (517–18).

It is not clear to me how Barth can be so concerned with associating the Bible's inspiration to the particular words of Scripture, and not merely to the "views and thoughts which evoke them," without presupposing that inspiration is an abiding quality of Scripture. Similarly, it seems to me that Barth's insistence that we must hear all of the words of the Bible "with the same measure of respect" is predicated on the assumption that these very words are divinely inspired.

A third and closely related objection to Barth's dynamic conception of inspiration is that, while Barth says we have no control over when God will choose to miraculously cause the Word to abide in the words of Scripture, nowhere in *Church Dogmatics* do we find Barth waiting or praying for this miracle to happen. He rather always presupposes that this has already taken place. It thus seems to me that the dynamic dimension of Barth's understanding of inspiration is a concept that plays no material role in how Barth actually engages with Scripture. And, as I'll argue below, I think this is a felicitous inconsistency.

Fourth, since Barth acknowledges that God, in his sovereignty and freedom, chose the original words of Scripture, I am puzzled as to why Barth thinks it would violate "the sovereignty and freedom of God" (513) to say that divine inspiration is an abiding quality of these words? If it didn't violate God's sovereign freedom to *originally* inspire these words, why should we think it would violate God's sovereign freedom if God sovereignly decided to *permanently* inspire these words?

In fact, it's not clear to me how God could *originally* inspire the words of Scripture without thereby *permanently* inspiring these words. If God chose these words over others, as Barth grants, then it will forever remain true that God chose these words over others. Is this not tantamount to acknowledging that divine inspiration is an abiding quality of Scripture?[6]

6. My point here is to demonstrate an inconsistency in Barth's thinking, not to endorse Barth's conception of "verbal inspiration." In part 2 of this work, I will argue that, while inspiration is an abiding quality of Scripture, a cross-centered conception of inspiration requires us to abandon the claim that the Spirit unilaterally chose the particular words found in Scripture.

A fifth problem with Barth's dynamic conception of divine inspiration is that, as much as Barth insists that God objectively speaks to us when he chooses to reveal God's Word in the words of Scripture, it seems to me that his dynamic conception of inspiration is actually entirely subjective. Because Barth collapses the distinction between objective reality and the subjective experience of reality when it comes to the inspiration of Scripture, Barth's framework would never allow a person to claim God has spoken until they have heard God speaking *to them*.

G. W. Bromiley, who was one of the most esteemed translators of, and authorities on, *Church Dogmatics*, makes this point when he writes:

> It is all well to say we are dependent on God Himself speaking in his Word, but the fact remains that if inspiration is not complete until it takes place in the individual, then God does not speak unless He speaks to me, and this means in practice that the only real or important act of "inspiration" takes place subjectively in the recipient.

And he continues:

> For a true objectivity it is necessary to insist that although there has to be the speaking to me, God has in fact already spoken: "men of old spake as they were moved by the Holy Ghost."[7]

In my estimation, the subjectivity of Barth's dynamic conception of inspiration is damaging to apologetics and evangelism, for all the same reasons that Barth's fideism is damaging. Christians claim to hear God speak in the Bible while Muslims claim to hear God in the Quran and Mormons claim to hear God in the Book of Mormon. Others claim to hear God in the book of Urantia, while still others claim to hear God in the poetry of Walt Whitman, the music of Enya, the storytelling of Dostoyevsky, and so on.

Now, it's entirely possible that all these claims are both sincere and, in a sense, correct. Perhaps God is actually speaking

7. G. W. Bromiley, "Karl Barth's Doctrine of Inspiration," *Journal of the Transactions of the Victoria Institute* 87 (1955):66–80 (80).

through these diverse means. It wouldn't be surprising, given that God is always working to use anyone and anything to reveal Godself to people, to the degree that this is possible in any given situation. But whatever else we might want to say about the nature of biblical inspiration, the church has always confessed that it is *unique to the Bible*. However God may speak through other means, the Bible alone is God-breathed for the purpose of bringing people into a relationship with Jesus Christ.

Barth of course believes this. Unfortunately, his dynamic conception of inspiration, combined with his fideism, render him unable to distinguish his claim to hear God speak in Scripture from the cacophony of similar-sounding claims of people hearing God by other means. As I argued above, Barth simply can't provide any *reasons* why a person should see the Bible as being any different from any other means of alleged divine communication. He can only testify—which is precisely what everyone else is doing.

The sixth and final criticism I'd like to raise against Barth's dynamic conception of inspiration is that the logic that led Barth to this conception should have led Barth to a dynamic conception of *everything* we believe God has said and done. For example, if "God's sovereignty and freedom" requires us to believe that the Bible only becomes the inspired story of God when God decides to miraculously give people the ability and will to believe it is so, shouldn't this same "sovereignty and freedom" require us to accept that the cross only becomes the definitive revelation of God and the atoning sacrifice for the sin of the world when God decides to miraculously give people the ability and will to believe it is so?

Interestingly enough, Barth is famous for his intense emphasis on the objectivity of Christ's revelatory and salvific work on the cross, arguing—correctly, in my opinion—that everything Christ accomplished on the cross applies to all, *whether they acknowledge it or not*. Yet, to the best of my knowledge, Barth nowhere explains why God's "freedom and sovereignty" require a dynamic conception of inspiration, but not a dynamic conception of the Atonement.

Nor, to the best of my knowledge, does Barth explain why

God's "freedom and sovereignty" does not require a similar dynamic conception of the incarnation—a point that is rendered all the more important because Barth uses the traditional incarnation analogy to understand the divine and human dimensions of the Bible, as I noted in the previous chapter. I do not believe this analogy is well suited for Barth's actual position, for the doctrine of the incarnation holds that in Jesus, God *permanently* united Godself to humanity.

For Barth, therefore, Jesus is God incarnate whether people believe it or not. Yet, this is precisely what Barth *denies* of Scripture. If it didn't violate the "freedom and sovereignty" of God when God permanently united Godself to a particular human and when God permanently accomplished God's revelatory and saving work on the cross, why should we think it contrary to God's "freedom and sovereignty" for God to permanently bind Godself to a book God inspired?

* * *

There is an even more fundamental reason why Barth's use of the incarnation analogy was ill-advised, and this brings me to the third and final set of objections I wish to raise against Barth's theology of Scripture. It concerns what I consider to be single most significant oversight in this theology. Discussing this oversight will serve as an ideal springboard to begin unpacking the Cruciform Model of Inspiration, to which we now turn.

PART II

Cruciform Inspiration

9.

Epicenter

> The crucified Christ is the key for all the divine secrets of Christian Theology. —Jürgen Moltmann

> I decided to know nothing among you except Jesus Christ, and him crucified. —1 Corinthians 2:2

In one sense, you could say that the Cruciform Model of Inspiration begins where Barth's reflections on the inspiration of Scripture leave off. In this chapter I'll lay the foundation for my discussion of the Cruciform Model of Inspiration by pinpointing the spot where I believe Barth's thinking on inspiration most comes up short.

To begin, we've seen that Barth contends that "even in their function as witnesses, even in *the act of writing down their witness*," biblical authors "were real, historical men who were sinful in their action, and capable and actually guilty of error in their spoken and written word" (529, emphasis added). Barth is here granting that the full humanity of the Bible is reflected in the fact that it not only contains errors, it contains *sin*. Yet, for Barth, the presence of sin in Scripture is no more a hindrance to it bearing witness to Christ than are the mistakes, inaccuracies, contradictions, or morally questionable material in Scripture.

God clearly has no problem breathing God's self-revelation through human fallibilities and sin, according to Barth. I consider this insight to be one of the most distinctive aspects of Barth's theology of Scripture. It is precisely at this point, however, that Barth's analogical use of the incarnation to illuminate the divine and human dimensions of Scripture fails.

According to Scripture as well as the traditional teaching of the church, which Barth frequently affirms, *Jesus was sinless*.[1] If the divine and human dimensions of Scripture are to be understood along the lines of the divine and human dimensions of Jesus, it seems we should have expected this collection of writings to be sinless, which Barth agrees is not the case. What Barth needed was not just an analogy of how God revealed Godself by uniting Godself with our fallible humanity, but an analogy of how God reveals Godself by uniting Godself *with our sin*. And this, I submit, Barth would have had if he had based his understanding of the divine and human dimensions of the Bible not on an analogy with the incarnation, but on the event that fulfilled the purpose of the incarnation: namely, the crucifixion.

* * *

Barth himself came within a hair's breadth of grasping this insight. At one point, Barth says that "the miracle of which we speak when we say that the Bible is the Word of God" is "that sinful and erring men as such speak the Word of God." Barth notes that this creates an "offense" that faith alone can remove, adding that, "like the offense of the cross," this offense "is based on the fact that the Word of God became flesh" (529).

What Barth failed to notice, however, was that, unlike the incarnation, "the offense of the cross" is not just that the "Word of God became flesh." The offense of the cross is rather the declaration that the Word who united himself with our humanity in the incarnation went even further to unite himself with our sin and even with the God-forsaken curse that reflects all the self-destructive consequence of that sin![2] Hence Jesus cried out to the Father on the cross, "Why have you forsaken me?"[3] The cross thus demonstrates that God is perfectly capable

1. Heb 4:15.
2. 2 Cor 5:21; Gal 3:13.
3. Matt 27:46.

of breathing God's self-revelation *through human sin* and even through human *God-forsakenness*. As such, I believe it serves as a much better analogy for Barth's conception of biblical inspiration than the incarnation.

However, I'm not merely suggesting that Barth should have used the cross analogy because it fits his perspective on Scripture better than the incarnation, though I believe that is true. Rather, I believe Barth should have used this analogy because, as I'll now demonstrate, the NT itself holds up the cross as the ultimate fulfillment of the reason for which the Word became flesh and as the definitive revelation of God's true character. Barth correctly understood that Christ is the center to which all Scripture is intended to point. What he failed to adequately appreciate, however, was that the cross is the epicenter of this center.

In what follows, I will make the case that everything about Jesus, from his incarnation to his resurrection and ascension, is oriented around the cross.[4]

* * *

Before reviewing this material, however, I must briefly respond to a potential objection at this point. One could argue that the resurrection rather than the crucifixion should be considered the culminating point of Jesus's ministry, for Jesus's death obviously wouldn't have been either revelatory or salvific if he had not risen from the dead. This is of course true, but it is also vitally important that we understand that the meaning of Jesus's resurrection is centered *on the cross*.

Once the church inherited political power in the fourth and fifth centuries, the resurrection began to be thought of in triumphalist terms that contrasted it with the crucifixion. That is, the resurrection came to mean that Jesus suffered *so we don't have to*. And because he suffered for us, we can now live in the victory of Jesus's resurrection power.

This is a fundamental distortion of the understanding of the

4. On that note, I would like readers to recall from the introduction that, when I refer to "the cross" or "the crucified Christ," I am not referring to Jesus sacrificial death *in contrast* to the rest of his life and ministry. I am rather referring to the cross as the *culminating point* and thematic *through line* of Jesus's whole life and ministry.

resurrection in the NT and early post-apostolic church. The resurrection accomplishes a lot of things, according to the NT. It confirms that the crucified one was and is the fully divine and fully human Son of God. It confirms that, in Christ, God has defeated the powers of death and has in principle reconciled the entire creation, and all of humanity, back to God. And it confirms that the cross is the definitive revelation of God's true character.

But, according to the NT, the resurrection also confirms that the way of the cross—the way of other-oriented, self-sacrificial love—is ultimately victorious and is the way God wants God's people to live. Hence, the cross is held up not only as something God did *for* us but also as something we are called and empowered *to emulate*. This is why Jesus told his disciples that they must "pick up your cross daily and follow me."[5] So too, Peter says disciples must be willing to suffer, for "Christ . . . suffered for you, leaving you an example, so that you should follow in his steps."[6] Indeed, for Paul, the same power that raised Jesus from the dead is working in the heart of believers to empower them to be conformed to Christ's own cruciform character.[7]

For all these reasons, I agree with those scholars who argue that the cross and resurrection are best understood as two sides of one and the same event.[8]

* * *

Perhaps the best place to start our discussion of the centrality of the cross is with John, who summarizes Jesus's revelation of God

5. Luke 9:32; 14:27.

6. 1 Peter 2:21; cf. Eph 5:1–2.

7. Phil 3:10, cf. Rom 8:17; 2 Cor 1:5; Gal 6:12; Col 1:24; 2 Tim 1:8. For an insightful and comprehensive overview of the centrality of the cross for Paul's understanding of discipleship, see M. Gorman, *Cruciformity: Paul's Narrative Spirituality of the Cross* (Grand Ra[ids: Eerdmans, 2001; M. Gorman, *Apostle of the Crucified Lord: A Theological Introduction to Paul and His Letters* (Grand Rapids: Eerdmans, 2003).

8. See the sources cited in G. Boyd, *Crucifixion of the Warrior God: Interpreting the Old Testament's Violent Portraits of God in Light of the Cross*, 2 vols. (Minneapolis: Fortress, 2017) 1:161–71.

by proclaiming that "God is love."[9] John is saying God's essence is love. Love isn't just a verb God *does*. Love is a noun that God *eternally is*.

It's a perfectly wonderful passage, but the all-important question is: what is love?

Augustine conveniently defined *love* as an inner-disposition that didn't necessarily have any behavioral implications.[10] It was a convenient definition for a church that had recently accepted the invitation to help run the Roman empire, for this subjective definition allowed Christians to torture and kill political and/or religious enemies while still claiming to comply with Jesus's instruction to "love" them. And so, from Augustine on, Christians have sometimes tortured and murdered Muslims, Jews, Native Americans, heretics, witches, infidels, and even multitudes of other Christians in the name of love and under the banner of Christ.[11]

What Augustine and the violent tradition that followed him failed to notice was that John doesn't obfuscate the meaning of love. John instead gives us as concrete and as clear a definition of love as possible when he writes: "*This* is how we know what love is, Jesus Christ laid down his life for us." And from this John concludes, "we ought to lay down our lives for one another."[12]

When John proclaims that, "God is love," *this* is the kind of love he is referring to. He is saying that the love that characterizes God's eternal nature, and the love that God's children are called to extend to all others, *looks like the cross.* God's eternal nature is the kind of love that is willing to set aside the blessedness and privileges of being God, stooping to unite Godself with our humanity, and then stooping even further to unite Godself with our sin and our God-forsaken curse. The

9. 1 John 4:8.

10. *Against Faustus*, 22.76, cited in O. O'Donovan, J. L. O'Donovan, eds., *From Irenaeus to Grotius: A Sourcebook in Christian Political Thought, 100–1625* (Grand Rapids: Eerdmans, 1999), 118. On issues surrounding Augustine's subjective definition of love and its tragic consequences in Church history, see F. H. Russell, "Love and Hate in Medieval Warfare: The Contribution of Saint Augustine," *Nottingham Medieval Studies* 31 (1987), 108–24.

11. For a bibliography of works discussing the dark side of church history from a variety of perspectives, see https://tinyurl.com/y2oyupwn.

12. 1 John 3:16 (emphasis added).

love that God eternally is, and the love God has for us, is a selfless love that is oriented toward the well-being of others, even when they could not deserve it less. It's a love that is self-sacrificial and nonviolent, choosing to suffer at the hands of enemies and out of love for enemies rather than to inflict suffering on enemies. It's a love that chooses to bear the guilt and the deserved punishment of foes rather than to justly punish foes on account of their guilt.

The cross reveals that the love that characterizes God's eternal nature is a love that ascribes worth to others, at cost to oneself. In fact, it's a love that ascribes *unsurpassable worth* to others, at cost to oneself, for on the cross God paid an *unsurpassable price* to redeem us. When John defined the kind of love that God eternally is by pointing us to the cross, he demonstrated that the cross is the supreme revelation of God. But the logic of the cross confirms this as well.

On the cross, the all-holy God fully identified with our *sin*, and the perfectly united triune God fully identified with the God-forsaken curse that is intrinsic to all sin.[13] Which, as I noted in chapter 3, means that on the cross, God went to the unsurpassable extreme of experiencing *God's own antithesis*. In the words of Barth, on the cross, God "set Himself in self-contradiction."[14] Never in all eternity could God stoop further than God did for us on the cross, and the unsurpassable distance God crossed on our behalf reveals the unsurpassable perfection of the love that God eternally is and that God extends to us, which is why the cross must be considered to be the unsurpassable revelation of God and the quintessential expression of everything Jesus was about.

Not surprisingly, everything the NT says about the cross confirms this.

* * *

The supremacy of the revelation that took place on Calvary is powerfully illustrated in the Gospel of John. In chapter 12, we find Jesus in the Garden of Gethsemane, understandably wishing

13. 2 Cor 5:21; Ga; 3:13.

14. K. Barth, *Church Dogmatics* Vol IV/1, *The Doctrine of Reconciliation*, trans. G. W. Bromiley (Edinburgh: T & T Clark, 1956), 184.

he could avoid the terrible fate that awaited him. However, Jesus immediately expressed his resolve to go forward by saying; "No, it was for this very reason that I have come to this hour."

Then, with a view towards his crucifixion, Jesus exclaimed; "Father, glorify your name!" The voice of the Father then thundered from the sky: "I have glorified it and will glorify it again." Jesus went on to declare; "when I am lifted up from the earth, I will draw all people to myself." And just to make sure readers did not miss the central point, John added that Jesus "said this to show the kind of death he was going to die."[15]

Finally, when Jesus's arrest was just around the corner, he exclaimed, "Father, the hour has come; glory your Son so that the Son may glorify you."[16] This passage unambiguously identifies Jesus's crucifixion as the "hour" when he would be glorified by glorifying Father's "name." In ancient Jewish culture, to speak of a person's "name" was to speak about their character and reputation. So, Jesus and the Father are both indicating that the Father's character would most clearly shine forth—be "glorified"—when Jesus was crucified.

While everything Jesus did from his incarnation to his ascension reflected the Father's character, the Father was "most glorified through the . . . 'lifting-up' . . . of the Son," as Andrew Moody notes.[17] Which is precisely why Jesus identifies the "hour" as the "very reason" he had come into our world. Since the cross was the supreme glorification of the Father, the many other lesser ways Jesus glorified the Father should be understood as anticipating, and pointing toward, this culminating event. Hence, as I've already mentioned, the cross should be understood as the through line of Jesus's entire ministry.

On this note, it's significant that, when the resurrected Jesus "explained . . . all Scriptures concerning himself" to the disciples on the road to Emmaus, it was primarily to demonstrate that

15. John 12:27–8, 31–33.

16. John 17:1.

17. A. Moody, "That All May Honour the Son: Holding Out for a Deeper Christocentrism," *Themelios* 36/3 (2011), 403–14 [414n437]. The original has "through" italicized. So argues C. S. Keener, *The Gospel of John*, 2 vols (Peabody, MA: Hendrickson, 2003) 2: 1147; R. Bauckham, *God Crucified: Monotheism and Christology in the New Testament* (Grand Rapids: Eerdmans, 1998), 63–68.

"the Messiah [had] *to suffer* these things."[18] And later, when Jesus "opened" the "minds of the apostles so they could understand the Scriptures," it was primarily so they could see that it declared that "the Messiah will *suffer* and rise from the dead on the third day."[19]

We should therefore not merely confess that all Scripture is God-breathed for the purpose of bearing witness *to Christ*; we should more specifically confess that all Scripture is God-breathed for the purpose of bearing witness to the *crucified* Christ. For the cross is the culminating expression of everything Jesus was about, from his incarnation to his resurrection and ascension. As I've already said, if Jesus is the center of Scripture, the cross is its epicenter.

* * *

The centrality of the cross is evident in a multitude of other ways as well throughout the NT. For example, the Gospels are from the start so strongly oriented toward Jesus's crucifixion that one NT scholar famously defined the Gospels as "*passion narratives** with extended introductions."[20] It also tells you a lot about the centrality of the cross in Paul's thought that he uses "the Gospel" and "the message of the cross" interchangeably.[21] So too, an enemy of the Gospel was, for Paul, an "enemy of the cross."[22] For Paul, clearly, the cross was the essence of the Gospel.

Reflecting this same point, the cross is at the center of every one of Paul's short summaries of the Gospel that we find sprinkled throughout his Epistles.[23] In fact, so thoroughly did Paul identify the cross with the content of the Gospel that he

18. Luke 24:26–27 (emphasis added).

19. Luke 24:45–46 (emphasis added).

20. M. Kähler, *The So-Called Historical Jesus and the Historic Biblical Christ*, trans. C. E. Braaten (Philadelphia: Fortress, 1964), 80n11 (emphasis added).

21. 1 Chr 1:17–18, 23.

22. Phil 3:18.

23. E.g., Gal 1:4; 2:19–20; 3:13–14, 26–28; 4:3–6. See Gorman, *Cruciformity*, 75–94; N. T. Wright, *The Day the Revolution Began: Reconsidering the Meaning of Jesus's Crucifixion* (New York: HarperOne, 2016), 229–33; J. B. Green, "Nothing but Christ and Him Crucified: Paul's Theology of the Cross," in J. B. Green et al., eds., *The Death of Jesus in Early Christianity* (Peabody, MA: Hendrickson, 1995), 123–32.

could tell the Corinthians that he "decided to know nothing among [them] except Jesus Christ, and him crucified."[24] This remarkable statement presupposes that everything Paul needed to know about God and about people is found on the cross.

In fact, Paul comes very close to explicitly stating this very thing. Speaking about "those in Laodicea," Paul says, "I want their hearts to be encouraged and united in love, so that they may have all the riches of assured understanding and have the knowledge of God's mystery, that is, Christ himself, in whom are hidden all the treasures of wisdom and knowledge."[25] Similarly, we've seen that Paul identifies the crucified Christ as "the wisdom of God" several times.[26]

If indeed "all the treasures of wisdom and knowledge" are found the crucified Christ, then we clearly should look nowhere else to discern wisdom or knowledge about anything pertaining to God. In this light, Jürgen Moltmann is clearly on the mark when he states, "The crucified Christ is the key for all the divine secrets of Christian Theology"[27] And this, I submit, should include the divine secret of how God breathed all Scripture for the purpose of pointing people to the cross.

* * *

Lest anyone think the intense emphasis I'm placing on the cross is a novelty, you should know that I haven't said anything that Martin Luther hadn't already said. In fact, Luther applied Paul's resolve to know "nothing except Jesus Christ and him crucified" (1 Cor 2:2) to his reading of Scripture. Hence, he claimed to "see nothing in Scripture except Christ crucified."[28] Similarly, at

24. 2 Cor 2:2.

25. Col 2:2–3.

26. 1 Cor 1:18, 24, 30.

27. J. Moltmann, *The Crucified God: The Cross as the Foundation and Criticism of Christian Theology*, trans. R. A. Wilson, J. Bowden (Minneapolis: Fortress, 1993), 114.

28. *Luther's Werke, kritische Gesamtausgabe*, ed. J. F. K. Knaake et al., 127 vols (Weimar: H. Bōhlau), vol 4, 153, quoted in A. S. Wood, *Captive to the Word: Martin Luther, Doctor of Sacred Scripture* (Exeter, UK: Paternoster, 1969, 171. On the significance of 1 Cor 2:2 in Luther's theology, see G. Tomlin, *The Power of the Cross: Theology and the Death of Christ in Paul, Luther and Pascal* (Carlisle, UK: Paternoster, 1999), 176–78.

another point Luther applied Jesus's statement, "he who has seen me has seen the Father," (John 14:9) to the cross and drew the conclusion that "true theology and recognition of God are in the crucified Christ."[29] From this, Graham Tomlin rightly concludes that the cross was for Luther "the key hermeneutical principle in understanding Scripture."[30]

Yet, Luther's remarkable *crucicentric** approach to Scripture is not as exceptional as it might at first seem, for as a matter of fact, the cross has played a central hermeneutical role in the church's reading of Scripture.[31] I am, in this book, simply inquiring into what this quintessential revelation of God might teach us about biblical inspiration.

In any event, I trust that this brief survey suffices to demonstrate that the revelation of God on Calvary is the centerpiece of the good news proclaimed by the NT. I have applauded Barth's intensely Christocentric approach to Scripture and to theology in general, but in light of the emphasis the NT places on the centrality of the cross, I submit that a truly consistent *Christocentric* perspective on biblical inspiration must also be a *crucicentric* perspective. For this reason, I submit that our reflections on the nature of biblical inspiration shouldn't be anchored in the incarnation, as Barth and so many others throughout church history have tried to do. We should rather anchor them in the cross, which fulfills the purpose for which God became incarnate.

* * *

In the previous chapter I expressed my appreciation for the fact that Barth held that even the "most offensive and least assimilable" aspects of Scripture must be considered to be God-breathed and that we only truly understand what it means to confess the Bible to be God's inspired story "when we recognize its human imperfection in face of its divine perfection, and its divine perfection in spite of its human imperfection." As much

29. *Luther's Works*, ed. J. Pelikan, H. T. Lehmann, 55 vols (St. Louis and Philadelphia; Concordia/ Fortress, 1958–86), 1:53.

30. Tomlin, *Power of the Cross*, 173.

31. For references, see Boyd, *Crucifixion of the Warrior God*, 1:250–59.

as I appreciate this statement, I must now confess that I don't believe it goes far enough.

If the "most offensive and least assimilable" aspects of Scripture are just as much God-breathed as its most beautiful and most easily assimilable aspects, and if we are "to hear all [biblical author's] words with the same measure of respect" (517–18), then I submit that Barth should *not* have said that we recognize the Bible's "human imperfection *in face of* its divine perfection, and its divine perfection *in spite of* its human imperfection." He should have rather said that, "we recognize the Bible's human imperfection as *a reflection of* its divine perfection, and its divine perfection as *a reflection of* its human imperfection."

Here is where the analogy of the cross would have served Barth well. On the cross, God breathed the full revelation of Godself through God's fully human Son as he bore the sin and God-forsaken curse of the fallen human race. But we wouldn't say that the cross fully reveals God *in spite of* the humanity, the sin, and the God-forsaken curse that Jesus bore. To the contrary, the cross fully reveals God *precisely because* it reveals a God who, out of unfathomable love, was willing to stoop to an unsurpassable distance to enter into solidarity with our humanity, our sin, and our God-forsaken curse.

In other words, despite the fact that the sin and curse that Jesus bore were antithetical to God's true eternal nature, they nevertheless *contribute to* the self-revelation that God breathes through them. And if the sin and curse that Jesus bore *contribute to* God's fullest self-revelation on the cross, why should we not expect to find sinful, cursed, and erroneous material *contributing to* the God-breathed story of God that bears witness to and culminates on the cross?

Similarly, since on the cross God revealed God's supreme wisdom and power by stooping to enter into solidarity with our foolishness and weakness, thereby taking on a foolish and weak appearance, why should we not expect to find God doing the same in the Scripture, especially since God breathed Scripture for the ultimate purpose of pointing people to this foolish and weak-appearing cross?

It's an important question we'll explore in more depth in the following chapter.

10.

The Foolish and Weak Bible

> The majesty of God in His condescension to the creature—that is the most general truth always told us by the reality of Jesus Christ. —Karl Barth

> God's foolishness is wiser than human wisdom, and God's weakness is stronger than human strength. —1 Cor 1:25

There are four aspects of the revelation of God in the crucified Christ that I will be discussing in this and the following four chapters that have a bearing on how we think about the nature of God's breathing. The first of these is simply that, while the cross is the power and wisdom of God to believers, it looks weak and foolish to the world's way of thinking about power and wisdom.

* * *

I am fully aware that I'm dating myself by using this illustration, but the movie I have in mind is *Indiana Jones and the Last Crusade*, starring Harrison Ford. If you enjoy over-the-top adventure comedies and haven't yet seen this 1989 classic, you might want to check it out. However, if you think you might actually take me up on this advice, I suggest you immediately put this book down and go watch the movie because I'm about to spoil a dramatic part of its ending.

Throughout the movie, Indiana Jones is racing against the Nazis to find the Holy Grail, which is the supposed chalice Jesus drank from at the Last Supper. The Nazis are after this ancient chalice because they've heard it possesses magical powers, including the power to grant immortality to anyone who drinks from it. While it's clear Indiana Jones wouldn't mind becoming immortal, he's not chasing the Grail for that reason. He's just a nerd archeologist who is interested in preserving ancient artifacts while saving the world from wicked Nazis.

After overcoming numerous and seemingly impossible obstacles, Jones and the leader of the Nazi group—a rather irritating fellow named Donovan—finally discover the secret chamber that contains the coveted sacred chalice. The magical chalice is kept under watch by a very old and wise knight. Unfortunately, the two also discover that the chamber is full of an array of very different looking chalices, and the old, wise knight instructs each of them to choose which chalice they believe Jesus drank from and then drink from it. They only get one choice. "Choose wisely," the knight says in an overly dramatic eerie voice.

What the old wise knight failed to mention, however, was that if they drink from a wrong chalice, they would, for some undisclosed reason, spontaneously combust and end up a pile of incinerated dust. One might have thought that detail would have been worth mentioning.

The irritating Nazi draws the long straw, which meant he was the "lucky" guy who got to go first. Donovan proceeds to scan the chalices until his equally irritating and greedy girlfriend draws his attention to the biggest, shiniest, and most expensive-looking chalice in the chamber. He is enamored with its beauty. "Jesus was a king," he says to himself. "Surely he would have drunk from a chalice fit for a king!" Donovan dips the chalice in a pool of water and takes a sip. Within seconds he begins to age very quickly, and within a couple more he self-combusts in a spectacular manner befitting a Hollywood classic such as this.

For a moment, a stunned Indiana Jones silently stares at the pile of dust that once was Donovan. The silence is broken only when the old wise knight states in that same slow and overly dramatic voice one of the greatest understatements in Hollywood history: "He chose . . . *poorly*."

It's then Jones's turn. He studies the chalices for a bit and then chooses the smallest and crudest cup in the room. "Jesus was a carpenter," Jones says to himself. "This looks like a carpenter's cup!" He takers a sip and, low and behold, he doesn't incinerate! "You chose . . . *wisely*," the old wise knight says with a slight smile.

But just when you thought Indiana was in the clear. . . . Well, either you've seen the movie and know what happens next, or you haven't and therefore shouldn't learn any more about the ending from me.

* * *

I'd like us to now engage in an imaginative thought experiment.

Imagine that you are in Indiana Jones's shoes, but instead of searching for the long-lost Holy Grail, you are living in a world in which the Bible hasn't been seen for a thousand years, and you are in a race to find it. You enter the same sort of chamber as Jones did, but instead of finding it filled with an array of different-looking chalices, you find it filled with an array of different-looking Bible's, each claiming to be the one true divinely inspired story of God.

The eerie old knight informs you that you must choose from among this collection of Bibles which book you believe is the true, inspired story of God. But, in this imaginative exercise, let's suppose that this knight happens to know everything there is to know about each of these Bibles, and while he won't tell you which is the true Bible, he is willing to share any other information you might like to know about any particular Bible in the chamber to help you choose wisely.

As you scan this collection of Bibles, there is one that catches your eye. It is as impressive-looking a tome as you have ever seen or imagined. You take it down off the shelf, and as you marvel at its features, you ask the knight to tell you about it. "This book," he says with a wry smile, "is perfect in every way an ancient religious text could be perfect." And he continues:

> Its literary quality is consistently exceptional. Every aspect of this book is spiritually profound and timelessly insightful. And this book is completely free of any reflection of human fallibility. It contains no errors, contradictions, historical inaccuracies, or moral questionable depictions of God.

Would you not be strongly inclined to conclude that this book must be the true divinely inspired story of God? If a perfect God were to inspire a collection of writings, it would surely look like this perfect Bible, right?

But suppose that, just as you are about to choose this impressive-looking Bible, your eye catches another book in the chamber that piques your curiosity, but for the opposite reason as the impressive-looking Bible. This Bible is as unimpressive as the other was impressive. So you ask the knight to tell you about it.

> Unlike the impressive-looking tome, the literary quality of this ancient collection of writings is all over the map. This Bible is also filled with errors and contradictions, and while many of its writings stand up reasonably well to historical-critical scrutiny, other writings in this collection do not. And while this collection contains some timelessly insightful wisdom, much of its material is culturally bound, including some of its depictions of God.

Suppose this wise knight then placed this ordinary appearing Bible right next to the impressive-looking and perfect-in-every-way Bible. He then looks straight into your eyes and says, "One of these two books is the true divinely inspired story of God and the other is not. Choose . . . *wisely*."

Be honest. If you didn't know I was setting you up right now, which Bible would you be inclined to pick? If you're like the vast majority of people, you'd select the impressive-looking book. It just makes sense. And yet, had you made that commonsensical choice, you would have chosen "poorly," and for all the same reasons Donovan chose poorly. And you would by now have become a ghoulish pile of dust, just like Donovan.

* * *

Donovan's fatal mistake was assuming that, since Jesus was a king, he must have drunken from a chalice that was "fit for a king." It makes sense. Kings have always used their superior power to benefit themselves and their loved ones. They have always lived in opulent castles, worn the richest and most ornate clothing, eaten the finest food, and drunken the finest wine from the biggest, shiniest, and most expensive-looking chalices. Since this is how human kings have always behaved, it's understandable that people would assume that this is also how King Jesus must have behaved.

As a matter of fact, this is what the vast majority of people throughout human history have assumed about God/gods. Since the gods have the *most* power, people have assumed that the gods must enjoy the most privileges, possess the most wealth, enjoy the most comfort, and display the most opulent glory. And people have always assumed this because this is what *they* would do if *they* were a god. They would display their greatness by *appearing great* and enjoying all of the advantages that come with being divine. After all, what good is it to possess all the advantages of divinity unless you're going to enjoy them?

And yet, had you chosen the impressive-looking and perfect-in-every-way Bible, you'd have been dead wrong. For, as a matter of fact, while sections of the true Bible are truly magnificent, it is, on the whole, closer to the *un*exceptional Bible in our thought experiment than it is to the impressive-looking perfect Bible. Which just goes to show that, if there is one thing that is true about the God who is revealed throughout Jesus's cross-centered life and ministry, it's that God doesn't conform to our commonsense assumptions.

* * *

The oddness of the God whom Jesus reveals is evident from the moment he decided to become incarnate. In diametric opposition to the way earthly kings and pagan gods have always used their superior status, Jesus never used any of the advantages he possessed as the Son of God for his own benefit. "Though he was in the form of God," Paul says, he "did not regard equality with God as something to be exploited." Instead, out of love for us, this altogether unique divine king set aside all the privileges he had to be "born in human likeness."[1]

Doesn't this seem like a rather foolish thing for an omnipotent God to do?

Not only did this unusual king empty himself of all of his *divine* privileges, he emptied himself of most of the *human* privileges that earthly kings typically enjoy as well. Instead of being born into royalty, this matchless king was born as an illegitimate son of an unmarried, peasant teenager. Instead of enjoying a palace, or even just an ordinary home, this peculiar king was born in a filthy animal stable. And instead of being adorned in ornate royal clothing, this unprecedented newborn king had to be wrapped up in common rags. Thirty-some years later, he would be crucified, likely wearing nothing at all.

Instead of sleeping in a large and comfortable royal bed, this astonishing infant king had to find rest in an animal feeding troth. Instead of being welcomed into the world with a pageantry worthy of a royal dignitary, this idiosyncratic infant king is welcomed only by a handful of lowly shepherds and pagan astrologers. And instead of enjoying a safe and secure environment fit for a king, Mary and Joseph had to protect this extraordinary child king from Herod's murderous designs by fleeing as immigrants to Egypt.

From the start, Jesus turned all our assumptions of what a divine king is *supposed to* be like on their head.

* * *

God's assault on our commonsense assumptions continues throughout Jesus's ministry. Instead of enjoying wealth and comfort, Jesus spent three years wandering about as a homeless teacher who had to live off the generosity of others. And it wasn't with the high and mighty that Jesus most associated, as kings typically do. This curious king rather spent most of his time fellowshipping with, and ministering to, the weak, the afflicted, the marginalized, the oppressed, and those whom

1. Phil 2:5–6.

high society judged most harshly, such as prostitutes and tax collectors.

The counterintuitive nature of Jesus's ministry is reflected as well in many of his teachings. Jesus says counterintuitive things like: The first will be last and the last will be first. It's better to serve than to be served. It's better to give than to receive. Many who assume they are insiders on the things of God will find themselves on the outside, and many whom people generally assume are outsiders will find themselves on the inside. The poor are blessed while the rich are warned. The mighty are brought low while the lowly are raised up. The ungodly tax collector who longs for mercy is justified while the righteous Pharisee who regularly prays and tithes is not. The weak are made strong and the strong are made weak. You get the picture.

What all such teachings have in common is that they reveal just how little we can trust our common sense when it comes to thinking about God and the way God operates in the world. At every turn Jesus's teachings turn our commonsense assumptions on their heads.

* * *

The same holds true for the way Jesus lived. One of the most beautiful examples of Jesus modeling the upside-down kingdom he was inaugurating takes place at the Last Supper. As Jesus shared this meal with his disciples, John tells us that he knew "that the Father had given all things into his hands, and that he had come from God and was going to God."

So, what do you do when you know you possess all the power in the universe?

We know very well what *we* would do if we had that kind of power: whatever else we did, we would use our superior power to our own advantage. However, this isn't what Jesus did. Jesus "got up from the table, took off his outer robe, and tied a towel around himself." He then "poured water into a basin and began to wash the disciples' feet and to wipe them with the towel that was tied around him."[2] Knowing he'd been given all

2. John 13:1–6.

authority, Jesus took on the role of a humble servant and washed the dirty smelly feet of his disciples—disciples whom he knew would abandon him and, in the case of Peter, explicitly deny him before the morning sunrise.

Clearly, unlike all human-imagined deities, the God revealed in Jesus Christ doesn't prefer to reveal his greatness by appearing great. God rather prefers to reveal God's greatness by divesting Godself of God's innate privileges in order to love, serve, and enter into solidarity with others. God prefers this because, as a matter of fact, God's greatness is reflected in the unfathomable depth of God's humble, servant-like, other-oriented, self-sacrificial love. When, in Christ, God humbles Godself in this manner, God is simply acting according to God's nature. For, as we've seen, God's very eternal nature is perfect cruciform love.

* * *

As is true of every significant aspect of Jesus's ministry, Jesus's revelation of the noncommonsensical cruciform God climaxes on the cross. Here God most clearly displayed the greatness of God's holiness by stooping to fully identifying with our sin, and here God most clearly revealed the radiance of God's glory by stooping to bear our shame.

On the cross, God most brilliantly displayed God's wisdom by stooping to appear foolish, and on the cross, God most unambiguously revealed the true nature of God's power by stooping to appear powerless. On the cross, God most spectacularly revealed God's unfathomable beauty by stooping to appear ugly, and on the cross, God most unambiguously revealed the perfection of God's loving tri-unity by entering into complete solidarity with the God-forsaken consequences of our sin. On the cross, God revealed the unsurpassable perfection of God's love by stooping an unsurpassable distance because this is what we needed him to do.

The cross, in sum, is the quintessential expression of everything Jesus was about, for everything Jesus was about reflects God's true cruciform character and will.

* * *

This brings us back to this fundamental point: If the cross reveals what God is truly like, it must be considered the quintessential expression of what God has always been like. It must, therefore, also be considered the perfect expression of, rather than an exception to, the way God generally operates in the world, a point Paul confirms when he announces that the cross is the wisdom and power of God. In this light, if we're basing our understanding of divine inspiration on the cross, as we should, how could we ever conclude that God must reveal God's greatness by breathing an impressive-looking book, or that God must reveal God's wisdom by breathing an exceptionally wise book?

Or, consider this same point from a different angle. The reason God appears weak, foolish, and guilty on the cross is because God was breathing a revelation of Godself through the Son, who out of love, had completely identified with the weakness, foolishness, and guilt of the human race. While the cross is of course a singular historical event, it nevertheless reveals the way God has always been, as I previously mentioned. This means that God has *always* been a God who reveals Godself by identifying with the weakness, foolishness, and guilt of the human race.

In this light, when we consider what is involved in the inspiration of Scripture, shouldn't we expect that it too will sometimes involve God stooping to identify with the weakness, foolishness, and guilt of those whom God is breathing God's self-revelation through? To think otherwise, it seems to me, is to suggest that the way God breathed God's fullest revelation on the cross is completely *unlike* the way God breathed the story of God that bears witness to the cross, which is tantamount to denying that the cross reveals what God has always been like.

* * *

This brings us to the second of four aspects of the cross that I believe can help illuminate our understanding of the nature of God's breathing. Over the following two chapters we'll discuss the curious fact that the God, who is inherently relational, is relational in everything God does, including God's breathing.

11.

Cruciform Breathing

> Teamwork begins by building trust. And the only way to do that is to overcome our need for invulnerability. —Patrick Lencioni

> Two are better than one. . . . And though one might prevail against another, two will withstand one. A threefold cord is not quickly broken. —Ecclesiastes 4: 9, 12

Steve is the Senior Pastor of a church that averages around 1500 attendees per weekend. Steve is one of those irritatingly gifted people who seem to be pretty good at just about everything they do. There is a danger in possessing such giftedness, however. You can be tempted into believing that your ideas about the way everything should be done are always the best ideas about the way everything should be done. And this, in turn, can transform you into something of a control-freak.

Unfortunately, Steve had succumbed to this temptation. In his church, it was pretty much Steve's way, or the highway. The employees and volunteers at Steve's church were expected to carry out Steve's visions, plans and instructions for each ministry, never to *contribute* to, or *give feedback* on, these visions, plans and instructions. The result was that the employees and volunteers at Steve's church felt like they were little more than cogs in the wheel of Steve's ambitions. All the talent, creativity, ideas, passion, and inspiration that these people had to offer went untapped. And since few people enjoy being a cog in someone else's wheel, there was a constant turnover of staff and volunteers at Steve's church, which in turn resulted in a constant turnover of attendees.

There is a lot that many would find attractive about Steve's church. Steve is an outstanding, insightful, and very humorous communicator. The worship service is very energetic (enhanced by an excellent rock band and multicolored flashing lights as well as fog). Their children's program is second to none, at least when it comes to making sure children want to come back the following week. And organizationally, Steve's church runs like a well-oiled machine.

Because of its impressiveness, Steve's church gets far more visitors each week than any other church in his city (at least that's the word on the street), but the only people who end up sticking around for very long are people for whom church is nothing more than a weekend service. People who want to use their talent, creativity, ideas, passion, and/or inspiration to make a difference in the world never last long in Steve's church.

However multitalented they may be, great leaders know the importance of empowering others and of treating people like *people* instead of cogs. In this chapter, we'll see that God is a truly great leader, even when God is breathing revelations of Godself. This brings me to the second of the four aspects of the cross that are significant to our understanding of how God breathes. It concerns the fact that when God breathed this definitive revelation on the cross, God *didn't do it alone.*

* * *

The vast majority of evangelicals adamantly reject the dictation model of inspiration, which holds that God virtually dictated every word of Scripture. In this view, the biblical authors whom God breathed through contribute nothing to what is produced as a result of God's breathing. Hence, every single word in the Bible is exactly as God wanted it, according to this view. I know of no academically respected scholar who espouses this view, for the simple reason that it's not hard to prove this view wrong, as I'll discuss below.

While almost everyone dismisses the dictation theory, however, it nevertheless seems to me that most Evangelicals as well as many others assume that God's breathing is a *unilateral* activity. God alone determines what is produced as a result of God's breathing. Which is why so many assume that the Bible must reflect God's own perfection.

It's not hard to see why people tend to assume God's breathing is a unilateral activity, since this is how all able-bodied persons breathe. Under normal circumstances, you don't need anyone's help breathing. Here again, however, we must be careful to guard against the ever-present temptation to project our commonsense assumptions onto God.

The fact of the matter is that, if we anchor our thinking about the nature of God's breathing in the crucified Christ, who embodies the entire treasure of God's wisdom, and if we reflect carefully on how this revelation came about, we can see that God's breathing is not unilateral; rather, it reflects God's relational, other-oriented, cruciform character. More specifically, when God breathed God's decisive self-revelation on the cross, it involved the Spirit *acting toward humanity*, but it also involved the Spirit humbly allowing the people she breathes through to *act toward God* and to thereby condition what was produced as a result of God's breathing.[1]

* * *

I know this is not the usual way people talk about divine inspiration, so let me break it down a bit.

To begin, the revelation of God in Jesus's cross-centered life and ministry clearly involved God acting *toward us*. God was acting toward humanity when God took the initiative of conceiving and implementing the cross-centered plan of salvation. God was also acting toward humanity when God raised up Abraham, worked through Israel, and, in partnership with humans, breathed the story of God's redemptive activity in our world.

1. I discuss why I use the feminine pronoun when referring to the Spirit in the introduction.

God was also dramatically acting toward humanity when God the Son emptied himself of his divine advantages to become a human, and at a juncture in history when circumstances rendered it certain that he would get crucified. And God was further acting toward humanity when Jesus taught about, and demonstrated, the reign of God with "signs and wonders" for three years. So too, God was acting toward humanity when Jesus forced the hand of the religious establishment to set things in motion that would result in his crucifixion.

Moreover, God was acting toward humanity when the Father "delivered Jesus over" to wicked humans and when the Son offered himself up, thereby, allowing people to afflict him with all the violence that was in their hearts. Similarly, God was acting toward humanity when God raised Jesus from the dead, thereby validating "the message of the cross." And, finally, God was acting toward humanity when God sent the Spirit to open people's eyes to the truth of who Jesus is and what Jesus's cross-centered life and ministry accomplished.

But the definitive revelation that God breathed through the crucified Christ didn't *only* involve God acting toward humanity. It also involved God humbly allowing humanity to *act toward God* and to thereby condition what was produced as a result of God's breathing. For starters, God was allowing humanity to act toward God and to condition how God appeared in the story of God when the Word became flesh. For the first time ever, and from now on into eternity, God's experience of God's own triune self would include the Son's experience of being a full human. By means of the incarnation, God has allowed humanity to permanently condition God's own experience of Godself.

Moreover, God was allowing humanity to act toward God whenever Jesus allowed people to impact him. Jesus's tender love for busy Martha; his tears over his deceased friend, Lazarus; his sorrow over the stubborn rich young ruler; his frustration over Peter's false bravado; his anger toward religiously abusive hypocrites; his delight in little children; and his amazement at the faith of a Centurion, to give just a few examples, all reflect various ways God incarnate allowed people to act toward him and affect him.

The same holds true for all the humiliation Jesus endured in the course of his Passion as well as for all the horrific violence that was inflicted on him. While it fell within God's plan of salvation to allow all this to happen, and, as the Son, to experience all this happening, it nevertheless remains true that all of the violence involved in Jesus's crucifixion was carried out by humans, operating under the influence of fallen powers.

Finally, and most significantly, in the crucified Christ, God allowed the sin and curse of humanity to act upon him and to condition how God appeared as a result of God's breathing. And this is precisely why God appears on the cross to be a guilty, God-forsaken, weak, foolish, crucified criminal.

* * *

When I say that God's breathing is relational, I am referring to this *mutually influential* dimension of God's breathing. God *acts*, but because God acts by means of influence rather than coercion, God also allows Godself to be *acted upon*. What gets produced as a result of God's breathing, therefore, is dependent not only on how God acts toward humanity but also on how God allows humanity to act toward God.

While it might initially seem puzzling, if not downright foolish, for an all-powerful God to allow fallen humans to condition the outcome of God's breathing, there are six interrelated and mutually reinforcing theological considerations that support it. The first three of these I'll discuss in the remainder of this chapter, while the remaining three will be covered in the next.

* * *

First, on one level, the relational conception of God's breathing is perfectly obvious. Even dictation theorists must acknowledge that each canonical writing reflects the personality, style, perspectives, culture, as well as the strengths and weaknesses of its human author. This is not what you'd expect if God unilaterally determined every word of the Bible, which is precisely why almost everybody rejects the dictation theory.

Paul's Greek tends to be better than Mark's, for example, though both of their writings are equally God-breathed, and despite the fact that I'm pretty sure God knows how to write in perfect Greek were God interested in unilaterally producing a work that was impressive in this respect. If a God-breathed book contains sections with mediocre Greek, this can only indicate that God humbly allowed the imperfect writing skills of an author to act upon God and to thereby condition what came about as a result of God's breathing. To this degree, at least, everyone must admit that God's breathing is relational.

Consider a statement Paul made in the course of encouraging the Corinthians to be less divisive. Paul was concerned that some Corinthian Christians were identifying themselves as followers of different teachers—Paul, Apollos, Cephas—instead of as followers of Christ. And, apparently, some were doing this on the basis of which teacher baptized them. To this Paul says, "Has Christ been divided? Was Paul crucified for you? Or were you baptized in the name of Paul? I thank God that I baptized none of you except Crispus and Gaius, so that no one can say that you were baptized in my name."[2]

Thus far Paul sounds confident, perhaps even a little proud, that he baptized next to no one at Corinth. But then Paul suddenly realizes that his claim to have only baptized Crispus and Gaius is mistaken. (So much for inerrancy!) Upon reflection, Paul has to acknowledge that he "did baptize also the household of Stephanas." However, Paul apparently realized that even this corrected memory was probably incomplete, for he immediately adds, "beyond that, I do not know whether I baptized anyone else."[3]

If you embrace the plenary inspiration of Scripture, as I do, then this passage must be considered to be as God-breathed as any other passage within the canon. Yet, I also believe this passage clearly illustrates how God's breathing involves God not only *acting toward* Paul, but also God allowing Paul, with his

2. 1 Cor 1:13–14.
3. 1 Cor 1:16.

imperfect memory, to act *toward God* and to thereby condition what was produced as a result of God's breathing. If Paul had a better memory, or maybe if he had simply gotten a better night's sleep the night before, God's story may not have included these self-corrections.

The fact that Scripture includes this self-correction reflects the humble beauty of a God who feels no need to perfect people before the Spirit breathes revelations through them.

* * *

It's impossible to deny that God accommodated the distinct personalities, the limited abilities, the particular circumstances, and the limited perspectives of biblical authors when God breathed through them to contribute to God's story. Yet, as we saw throughout part 1, to preserve their doctrine of inerrancy, many evangelicals draw a line in the sand when it comes to fallible and fallen aspects of a biblical author's personality or belief system. We also saw that others give up trying to defend the inerrancy of all Scripture but nevertheless try to discern an error-free safe zone that is distinct from the Bible's fallen and fallible material.

Once we anchor all our thinking about inspiration in the crucified Christ, however, we can see that there is no need, and no basis, for trying to defend inerrancy, whether of the whole Bible or for select material within the Bible. For on the cross, God breathed the definitive revelation of Godself through one who bore all that was broken, sinful, and cursed about humanity. Which suffices to demonstrate that Barth was right: God clearly has no problem breathing self-revelations through broken, sinful, and cursed people.

* * *

The second consideration that supports the relational conception of God's breathing is that this conception is consistent with, if not required by, the traditional teaching that God is an eternal community of three divine Persons, each of whom is utterly poured out in selfless love for the other two. This teaching has traditionally been known as the *perichoresis,** or the "mutual indwelling," of the three Persons of the Trinity.

While each divine Person is distinct from the other two, according to this teaching, each perfectly gives themselves away in love to the other two, and each fully embraces the total self-giving of the other two. So complete is the eternal self-giving love of the triune God that, at least according to the *Cappadocian fathers** who first formalized this teaching in the fourth century, the distinctness of each divine Person is wholly defined by their unique other-oriented relationship with the other two.

If we accept this traditional (and, I might add, profoundly beautiful) understanding of the Trinity, then we must consider God's very being to be an eternal dance in which each of the three divine Person's *acts toward* the other two by completely pouring themselves out toward them, and each divine Person allows the other two *to act toward them* by completely opening themselves up to them. God's very essence thus involves an eternal pouring out as well as an eternal opening up. In other words, *the unsurpassable love that is God's eternal nature is a love that eternally acts toward another while allowing the other to act toward God.*

And when God's loving, acting-and-being-acted-upon nature is turned outward toward a fallen world, *it looks like Jesus Christ crucified.* Which is to say, the manner in which Jesus lovingly set aside his divine advantages to empty himself (*kenosis*) and become a full human being, replicates the humble, other-oriented, outpouring of selfless love that eternally defines the Trinity. So too, the manner in which God selflessly entered into complete solidarity with our sin and our curse on the cross replicates the unsurpassable perfection of the poured-out-ness of the three divine Persons towards one another.

In short, the manner in which God completely poured Godself out for us on the cross replicates the manner in which God is completely poured out within God's own eternal triune being. Thus, the cross is simply what it looks like when God loves the way God eternally loves, but now in relation to a fallen and oppressed creation. Which, again, is simply to say that the cross is what it looks like when God's eternally loving acting-and-being-acted-upon nature turns outward to rescue and beautify our perishing world.

Which leads directly to this question: Since the cross replicates God's eternal acting-and-being-acted-upon nature, and since God breathed Scripture for the ultimate purpose of pointing us to the cross, how can we *not* conceive of God's breathing as a process of God acting and allowing Godself to be acted upon?

Once we embrace this relational conception of God's breathing, all the fallible and fallen aspects of the God-breathed story of God stop being problems. Indeed, understood in light of the cross, these former problems become testaments to the truth that the Spirit has always allowed the imperfections and sin of people to act upon God and to therefore condition what results from God's breathing, just as happens in a *paradigmatic** way on the cross.

* * *

The third consideration I'd like to offer in support of the mutually influential conception of divine inspiration is that, throughout the inspired story of God, God almost always accomplishes God's purposes in partnership with others—which is precisely what we should expect, given that God's eternal nature is relational.

You can see this right from the get-go. Obviously, Yahweh could have unilaterally exercised dominion over the earth and animal kingdoms. Instead, Yahweh commissioned the newly created humans to serve as God's viceroys on earth by exercising loving dominion over the earth and animal kingdom. This is why Yahweh empowers Adam to name the animals and waits "to see what he would name them."[4] Yahweh clearly intended to rule over the earth and animal kingdom, but God just as clearly did not want to do this alone or unilaterally.

This is what we find throughout God's story. In fact, after the creation of the world, there is very little that God does alone and unilaterally. And, as I've argued elsewhere, even in narratives in which it may initially seem that God is acting alone, especially to

4. Gen 2:19–20.

bring a nation or people group under judgment, a closer reading of the biblical narrative almost always provides hints that God was actually working through other agents, whether human or angelic.[5]

Paul captures God's partnership with humans when he describes Christians as God's coworkers (*synergeo*).[6] This word literally refers to one who works or expends energy (*ergos)* alongside of (*syn*) another. This means that we humans are to bring our own *ergos*—our heart, time, talent, resources—alongside God's *ergos* to accomplish God's plans. It means we genuinely contribute something to the way God's plans get accomplished. It means we possess genuine say-so to affect what comes to pass in any moment, say-so that genuinely influences the shape God's providential work takes. It means our choices make a difference both to God and to the world. It means that things genuinely hang in the balance on what we choose to do and not do.

The very fact that God's story is almost entirely a story of God's partnerships, combined with the fact that God allows God's imperfect partners to influence the shape God's providential activity takes, gives us yet another reason to think of God's breathing along the lines of a mutually influential partnership. The entire biblical narrative reflects the Spirit influentially acting toward humans, but it also reflects the Spirit humbly allowing the condition and circumstances of the humans she was partnering with to breath God's story to influentially act toward her and to thereby condition what was produced as a result of God's breathing.

Yet, we have not gotten to the bottom of why the relational God does not exhaustively control the agents God breathes through. There are three further important considerations that clarify this, as we'll see in the following chapter.

5. G. Boyd, *Crucifixion of the Warrior God: Interpreting the Old Testament's Violent Portraits of Christ in Light of the Cross*, 2 vols. (Minneapolis: Fortress, 2017), 2:851–90, 1121–92.

6. 1 Cor 3:9; 2 Cor 6:1.

12.

Cruciform Power

> To show your weakness is to make yourself vulnerable. To make yourself vulnerable is to show your strength. —Cassi Jami

> Love is patient; love is kind; love is not envious or boastful or arrogant or rude. It does not insist on its own way; it is not irritable or resentful; it does not rejoice in wrongdoing, but rejoices in the truth. It bears all things, believes all things, hopes all things, endures all things —1 Corinthians 13:4–7

A beautiful, unmarried girl in an ancient Buddhist village became pregnant. Feeling the judgment of their neighbors, her parents angrily insisted their daughter tell them who the father was. The young girl initially resisted, but under the relentless insistence of her parents, the girl finally pointed her finger at Hakuin, a Buddhist monk whom the entire village had always revered for his pure life.

When the outraged parents confronted Hakuin with their daughter's accusation, he simply replied, "Is that so?"

Word of Hakuin's alleged misdeed spread quickly, and he instantly became the town pariah. No one would talk to, or even make eye contact with, this once-revered monk. Once the child was born, the young girl's parents brought the baby to Hakuin and insisted that he take full responsibility for raising this child, since he was its father.

"Is that so?" Hakuin said as he calmly accepted the child into his home.

For many months this Buddhist monk tenderly cared for this child as though she was his own, until one day the daughter found she could no longer live with the lie she had told. She confessed that the real father was a young man in the village whom she had been trying to protect. The parents immediately went to Hakuin, and with profuse apologies they explained what had happened.

"Is that so?" Hakuin said as he handed the child back to them with a smile.

This Buddhist story is meant to illustrate how an enlightened person accepts things as they are and is unconcerned with the judgments of others. But for just this reason, this story also illustrates a unique kind of strength. It takes strength to choose to bear the sin and shame of another and to thereby appear guilty and suffer the judgments of others when you know you are perfectly innocent. It is the kind of unique strength that Jesus displayed on the cross and, I believe, that God displays when God breathes revelations of Godself.

* * *

This brings me to the fourth of the six considerations that support the relational conception of God's breathing. It concerns the fact that Paul declares that "the cross is the power of God."[1] This is arguably the single most stunning revelation in all Scripture. When God flexes God's omnipotent bicep, Paul is saying, it looks like Jesus setting aside the advantages of being God, becoming a vulnerable human, and taking on the guilt and shame of the very people who are crucifying him, which, ultimately, is all of us.

This conception of divine power is so contrary to our normal, fallen, coercive ways of thinking about power that even the vast majority of Christians throughout church history haven't believed it! In diametric opposition to the kind of coercive power that fallen humans (including most Christians) have

1. 1 Cor 1:18, 24.

always ascribed to God/gods, the cross reveals that God's power is nothing other than the influential lure of God's beautiful, other-oriented, self-sacrificial, loving character.

In keeping with the perichoretic loving essence of God, discussed in the previous chapter, the cross reveals that God relies on a loving kind of power that wins the hearts of people, if they are willing, but that would never coerce the hearts of people to make them willing. It's why Jesus claimed that he would "draw all people to [himself]" once he was "lifted up."[2] And it's why Jesus always left the decision about whether to follow him or not up to the people who needed to make that decision.

God's power, in short, is nothing other than the beauty of God's loving character put fully on display, which is precisely what the cross does. When one comes under the grips of this loving power, such as Paul did, one feels compelled, but never coerced, to become a passionate coworker of God.[3]

* * *

In keeping with the kind of power humans have always projected onto God/gods, *classical theologians** have always associated God's power with God's supposed "immutability" (God never changes) and "impassibility" (God has no passions and does not suffer). If immutability merely posited that God's perfect *character* never changes, or if impassibility merely posited that God's emotions never get out of control, there would be no problem. Some scholars have attempted to argue that this is all that the early church fathers meant with these concepts, but more than a few of us think these scholars are involved in wishful thinking.[4] Among other things, if that is all that

2. John 12:32.

3. 2 Cor 5:14. The word *synechô* in this passage means "to compel" or "constrain", as it is usually translated. However, several translations (e.g., ESV, NLT, NASB) translate *synechô* as "to control," which goes too far, in my opinion. Even Paul's initial Damascus road encounter with the resurrected Lord, as powerful as it was, didn't control Paul. Hence, he later told king Agrippa that he "was not disobedient to that heaven vision" (Acts 26:19), which, of course, implies that Paul could have disobeyed that heavenly vision.

4. For several defenses, see P. Gavrilyuk, *The Suffering of the Impassible God: The Dialectics of Patristic Thought* (Oxford: Oxford University Press, 2004); T. G.

theologians from the third century on ever meant by immutability and impassability, why did so many of the early church thinkers go to such great lengths to avoid ascribing Jesus's suffering *to his divinity*?

In any event, if we anchored all our thinking about divinity in the crucified Christ, I submit it would never occur to us to suspect that Jesus's divinity must be "above" the capacity to change and to suffer.[5] The Word *became* flesh and then *became* our sin and our curse![6] If this doesn't reveal a God who is capable of change and capable of suffering, then what *does* it reveal?

I submit that the cross reveals that God's power is precisely God's loving willingness to be profoundly impacted by others and to suffer at the hands of (and for the sake of) others. It's a kind of power that grants, and then respects, the personhood and the say-so of others. It's thus a kind of power that is "patient" and "kind," that "does not insist on its own way," that "bears all things, believes all things, hopes all things," and "endures all things."[7] It's the opposite of the coercive I-get-things-my-way power the world perpetually lusts after.

It's true that everything I just said about God's power—that

Weinandy, *Does God Suffer?* (Notre Dame: University of Notre Dame Press, 2000); G. Bray, *The Personal God: Is the Classical Understanding of God Tenable?* (Carlisle, Cumbria, UK: Paternoster, 1998); J. Dolezal, *All That Is in God: Evangelical Theology and the Challenge of Classical Theism* (Grand Rapids: Reformation Heritage Books, 2017).

5. I put "above" in ironic warning quotes since I deny the assumption that a being who wasn't able to be impacted by others or to suffer or to have strong emotions is superior to, "above," a being who is open to being impacted by others and to suffering and having strong emotions. I would say the same thing for the classical theistic assumption that a being who did not experience sequence (is "above" time) is superior to a being who does experience sequence. For several critiques of classical theism, see J. Moltmann, *The Crucified God: The Cross of Christ as the Foundation and Criticism of Christian Theology* (Minneapolis, MN: Fortress, 1993); J. Sanders, *The God Who Risks: A Theology of Divine Providence* (Downers Grove, IL: InterVarsity Academic, 2007); P. Fiddes, *The Creative Suffering of God* (London/Oxford: Clarendon Press, 1988;) J. Hallman, *The Descent of God: Divine Suffering in History and Theology* (Minneapolis, MN: Fortress, 1991); I. A. Dörner, *Divine Immutability* (Minneapolis: Fortress Press, 1994 [1956–58]); C. Hartshorne, *The Logic of Perfection and Other Essays in Neoclassical Metaphysics* (LaSalle, IL: Open Court, 1962).

6. John 1:14; 2 Cor 5:21; Gal 3:13.

7. 1 Cor 13:4–7.

is, that it's "patient" and "does not insist on its own way"—Paul originally said about love. But since the cross is presented as the perfect revelation of both God's love and God's power, whatever can be said of one can be said of the other. Indeed, since Jesus's cross-centered life and ministry reveal that God's eternal essence *is* mutually influential, other-oriented love, as we saw in the previous chapter, I agree with those theologians who argue that we must consider God's power, along with every other attribute of God, to simply be *an expression of God's love*.[8]

Hence, if we consider the cross to be the paradigmatic example of how God breathes, I believe we ought to accept that, whatever else we might want to say about the kind of power that God exerts when God breathes forth God's story, it must be an influential kind of power that respects the personhood of others rather than a coercive kind of power that does not. Hence, it must be a power that allows those with whom God is partnering to contribute to, and thus condition, what gets produced as a result of God's breathing.

* * *

The fifth consideration that I believe supports the relational conception of God's breathing concerns the nature of free will.

When God gives an agent a certain degree of say-so to influence what comes to pass, God is basically giving this agent the capacity to freely choose to go this way *or that way*.[9] However, if God were to unilaterally—and therefore coercively—determine that an agent will go *this* way *rather than* that way, this would simply demonstrate that, as a matter of fact, God *hadn't* actually given this agent the ability to go this

8. E.g., P. Kreeft, *Knowing the Truth of God's Love: The One Thing We Can't Live Without* (Ann Arbor, MI: Servant Books, 1988).

9. The concept of free will (or of "having 'say-so'") that I'm defending is called "libertarian free will." It contrasts with "compatible free will," which holds that free will is compatible with determinism. For several philosophical and/or theological defenses of libertarian free will, see T O'Connor, The Metaphysics of Free Will (New York: Oxford University Press, 2000); R. Kane, *The Significance of Free Will* (New York: Oxford University Press, 1996) G. Boyd, *Satan and the Problem of Evil: Constructing a Trinitarian Warfare Theodicy* (Downers Grove, IL: InterVarsity Academic, 2001).

way *or that* way. In other words, if God genuinely gives an agent the ability to freely choose to go this *or that* way, then, by definition, God *must* allow the agent to go *that* way if the agent so chooses, regardless of how much God might wish the agent would choose otherwise. The possibility of an agent deciding to go against God's will is the risk God must take in endowing agents with genuine say-so over what comes to pass.

What this all means is that free will is, by definition, *irrevocable*. God *can't* unilaterally revoke free will once it has been given for the same reason God can't create a married bachelor, a round triangle, a rock too heavy for God to lift, or a godly mass-murderer. These things are logical contradictions. They assert and deny the same thing, which means they assert nothing. It's thus no more a limitation on God to acknowledge that God *can't* override a free agent's free will than it would be to acknowledge that God *can't* render it false that I just wrote "render it false."

In this light, for God to endow an agent with a certain amount of say-so over what comes to pass *entails that* God has *irrevocably* endowed this agent with this amount of say-so over what comes to pass.[10] And this provides us with yet another reason why, when God decides to work to accomplish a plan or to breath a revelation of Godself by means of a human coworker, God always respects their personhood by honoring their say-so and allowing it to condition what God's breathing produces.

Of course, it was God alone who freely chose to endow humans with free will. In this sense we can say that God humbly *chooses* to respect the personhood of God's human partners and to accommodate their sin. A less loving, humble, self-secure and adventurous deity would have instead played it safe and stuck with a creation that could be unilaterally controlled. The loving God revealed on Calvary is anything but a play-it-safe deity, however. And once this God made the bold decision to create free agents, honoring this freedom is simply a matter of logical necessity, though every time God does this, it reflects on the love, humility, security, and adventurous nature of God's decision to populate the world with free agents.

10. For a more in-depth development of this argument and response to potential objections, see Boyd, *Satan and the Problem*, 178–206.

In this light, we may say that God relies on the influential power of love rather than coercive power not only because this is the only kind of power that is consistent with God's cruciform character, but also because this is the only kind of power that is consistent with loving and interacting with free agents.

Applying this insight to the nature of God's breathing, it is apparent that God acts toward God's authors by influentially working to reveal as much of God's true self *as possible*. And God accommodates the say-so of these authors *as much as necessary*, thereby allowing the spiritual condition of these authors, of God's people in general, to condition what results from God's breathing.

* * *

But, you may wonder, why would God take the risk of giving agents the say-so to go against God's will in the first place? Given the nightmarish suffering that humans have brought about, one might suspect that the previously mentioned play-it-safe deity might have been a wiser god.

The most common response to this question throughout church history is that God endowed humans with free will because God's chief goal for creation is to invite humans to participate in God's triune love, and *love must be freely chosen.* The same argument has traditionally been made for the free will of angels. I am in complete agreement with this traditional response. A coerced, manipulated, or preprogramed "love" isn't genuine love. Hence, if love is the goal, free will, and the potential for evil and suffering that comes with it, was the risk God had to be willing to take.

And on the cross, God paid that price in spectacular fashion.

* * *

The sixth and final consideration that I believe supports the relational conception of God's breathing concerns the simple fact that, if God enters into a relationship with people, it must be mutually influential, *for this is simply what it means to have a relationship with someone.*

A relationship in which one party has say-so to influence the other party but in which the second party has no say-so to influence the first is not a relationship; it's a *monopoly*. In a monopoly, one person is not genuinely relating *to* another. Instead, one person is relating to himself or herself *through* another. This dynamic doesn't change just because we're talking about a relationship with God. For God to have a relationship with *you*, there must be a *you* for God to have a relationship with. And that *you* must be somewhat autonomous from God, which means you must possess some of your own say-so to contribute to the relationship.

If at any given moment God decided to unilaterally override your autonomous say-so and determine everything about you, then, at least in that moment, God would not be having a relationship with you. For if God determined everything about you, there would be no *you* for God to relate to.

* * *

I can take this train of thought a step further by noting a subtle contradiction that I believe lies at the heart of Calvinism and all forms of *theological determinism*.* Theological determinism fails to realize that if *A* exhaustively determines *B*, then *B* is simply another name for *A*. In this case, the distinction between *A* and *B* is merely verbal, meaning that *B* is simply serving as another name for *A*. *B* can only be said to be *genuinely* distinct from *A* if *B contributes something* that *A* didn't already have and didn't unilaterally determine *B* to have. In short, *B* can be said to be distinct from *A* only to the degree that *B* has some element of autonomous say-so over and against *A*.

So too, people can only be said to be distinct from God, and God can only be said to genuinely relate to people, if people possess some degree of autonomous say-so over and against God. As I noted in the previous chapter, Paul says we are God's coworkers, which means we bring our own say-so into our relationship with God. Hence, if God was in a genuine relationship with those through whom God breathed God's story, then we must accept that God's interactions with them had to be noncoercive. However much the Spirit successfully influencing a given author in the direction of truth, the point at which a more intense influence would have become coercive is the point at which the Spirit humbly stoops to allow the limited and fallen state of the author she is breathing through to condition what is produced as a result of her breathing.

Love grants say-so to the other, and both love and logical necessity prevent it from being withdrawn. Which is why love is always mutually influential. And this provides yet another insight into why God stoops to accommodate the shortcomings of God's coworkers when the Spirit breathes through them as well as another reason why we ought not to be at all surprised when we discover that our God-breathed Bible reflects so much of the fallibilities of its human authors.

13.

Cruciform Accommodation

> This love of God is His grace. It is a love in the form of the deepest condescension. . . . It is a love which is merciful, making this movement, this act of condescension, in such a way that, in taking to itself this other, it identifies itself with its need, and meets its plight by making it its own concern.—Karl Barth

> Love covers a multitude of sins. —1 Peter 4:8

Thus far we have reflected on two of the four aspects of God's revelation on the cross that should impact our understanding of how God breathes. The first concerned the foolish and weak nature of God's breathing, and the second, which we covered in the previous two chapters, concerned the relational nature of God's breathing. We turn now to the third aspect of the cross that I believe should inform our conception of divine inspiration. It concerns the fact that the cross is the paradigmatic example of God stooping to accommodate the fallen and broken state of humanity and of creation.

* * *

I love the story of Elisha healing the leprosy of Naaman, the commander of the Aramaean army. Elisha sent a servant to tell Naaman, "Go, wash yourself seven times in the Jordan, and your flesh will be restored and you will be cleansed."[1] Though he had to fight through his pride to do it, Naaman reluctantly complied with Elisha's instructions, with the result that "his flesh was restored and became clean like that of a young boy."[2]

Naaman went back to Elisha and professed that he now knew "there is no God in all the world except in Israel."[3] Interestingly enough, Naaman then asked Elisha if he could "be given as much earth as a pair of mules can carry, for your servant will never again make burnt offerings and sacrifices to any other god but the Lord."[4] Throughout the ANE, people associated gods with particular territories, and this same perspective is reflected throughout the OT.[5] Naaman and Elisha thus naturally assumed that if Naaman was to henceforth worship Yahweh, the God of Israel, he would need to do it while standing on Yahweh's land. So, since Naaman had to return to Aram, he was asking to take some Israeli dirt home with him.

Elisha grants Naaman's request, but then Naaman makes another: "When my master enters the temple of Rimmon to bow down and he is leaning on my arm and I have to bow there also—when I bow down in the temple of Rimmon, may the Lord forgive your servant for this." Elisha simply replies, "Go in peace."[6] I think that is astonishing!

If Naaman had refused to bow to the idol of Rimmon, he would have been executed, or worse. Of course, Elisha could have told Naaman that torture and possible death are simply the price one must be willing to pay if they are going to devote themselves to Yahweh. Elisha also could have told him some of the stories in the Bible of Yahweh smiting people who bowed to foreign idols. Or he could have included the story of Yahweh ordering the extermination of entire populations throughout the land of Canaan just to protect the Israelites from being

1. 2 Kg 5:10.
2. 2 Kg 5:14.
3. 2 Kg 5:15.
4. 2 Kg 5:17.
5. E.g., Deut 12:30; 29:30; 2 Sam 7:23; 2 Kgs 17:33; 2 Chr 32:13–24; Micah 4:5; Zeph 2:11.
6. 2 Kg 5: 18–19.

influenced by their idolatry.[7] Instead, this holy prophet of Israel told Naaman not to worry about it!

Both Naaman and Elisha know that bowing before an idol, if only to save your own skin, is not ideal, which is why Naaman feels the need to ask for Elisha's forgiveness. But while this action misses the mark of God's ideal, it apparently was the best Elijah surmised he could hope for from Naaman. After all, by committing himself to worshipping and sacrifice to no other god but Yahweh, Naaman had already undergone a monumental faith-paradigm shift. And he had demonstrated his sincerity by preparing to haul a ton of Israeli dirt back to Aram in order to carry out this worship and sacrifice. To demand more than this, I suspect Elisha thought, would be too much.

And so, Elisha mercifully accommodated Naaman's understandable desire to avoid execution by pretending to worship the god Rimmon. In the same way, God accommodated Naaman's and Elisha's fallen and culturally conditioned belief that Yahweh could only be worshipped on Israeli soil.

In this chapter, we're going to find that God has been stooping to mercifully accommodate sin and weakness since the fall of humankind.

* * *

As paradoxical as it may sound, the cross is simultaneously the supreme example of God both accommodating, and judging, sin. More specifically, the cross is the supreme example of God stooping to embrace humanity, just as we are, hopelessly in bondage to the fallen powers and to our fallen nature. Yet, the cross is also the supreme example of God bringing judgment on sin by allowing its inherently self-destructive nature to run its course. And the cross functions in this paradoxical way because, on the cross, God allowed the sin of the world to run its full self-destructive course *on Godself*, in the person of Jesus Christ.

The cross thus reveals a God who loves us as we are, who utterly pours Godself out toward us by entering into total

7. E.g., Lev 18:24–25; Deut 9:5; 18:12.

solidarity with us as we are, and who chooses to suffer the death consequences of our sin on our behalf rather than to allow us to experience these consequences.

In short, on the cross, God suffers God's own judgment on sin in order to accommodate us in our sin.

* * *

I want to be very clear about what I am and *am not* saying here.

Many today believe Jesus had to die to satisfy the Father's just wrath against sin before the Father could forgive us. The assumption is that God's holiness demands that no sin can go unpunished. Someone has to pay for it! So either we humans pay for it by suffering forever in hell, or Jesus must pay for it by getting crucified (though I frankly have never understood how Jesus's temporary suffering sufficed to pay off our allegedly eternal debt). This view is known as the Penal Substitution view of the Atonement (PSA).

When I say the cross reveals a God who suffers God's own judgment on sin in order to accommodate us in our sin, I want to be clear that I am *not* advocating this view. Among the multitude of problems I have with this view, it doesn't allow God to ever really *forgive* people.[8] Forgiveness is about r*eleasing* a debt, not *collecting it from someone else*. Those who embrace PSA may celebrate that Jesus got them off the hook by (somehow) paying off their eternal debt, but they can't celebrate that God *forgave* them.

In my view, the problem that God needed to solve was not about how to reconcile God's holiness with God's desire to save sinners. The problem God rather needed to solve was how to "reconcile the world to himself."[9] The conflict, in other words,

8. There is a sustained critique of PSA throughout N. T. Wright, *The Day the Revolution Began: Reconsidering the Meaning of Jesus's Crucifixion* (New York: HarperCollins, 2016). See also B. Jersak and M. Hardin, eds., *Stricken by God? Nonviolent Identification and the Victory of Christ* (Grand Rapids: Eerdmans, 2006); J. Beilby and P. Eddy, *The Nature of the Atonement: Four Views* (Downers Grove, IL: InterVarsity Academic, 2006), 99–116; S. Chalke, *The Lost Message of Jesus* (Grand Rapids: Zondervan, 2003).

9. 2 Cor 5:19.

was not between God's holiness and God's love, but between God's love, which includes God's holiness, and the unreconciled state of the world.

According to Jesus and the authors of the NT, our world is estranged from God because our rebellion against God has subjected it to the oppressive and corrupting reign of Satan and "the powers."[10] Hence, Satan is called the "ruler of the world," the "god of this age," and "the principal power of the air" who "controls the entire world."[11] In bondage to the powers and our own corrupted nature, we are, apart from Christ, "dead in our sin" and "by nature, objects of wrath."[12]

I don't believe this means God is personally enraged toward people until they come to Christ. The primary conception of God's "wrath" or "judgment" in Scripture, and the only conception that is congruent with the nature of God's judgment revealed on the cross, is that it refers to God's decision to deliver people over to the self-destructive-consequences that are inherent in their sin.[13] Hence, Scripture often describes God's judgments as a matter of God allowing people to *punish themselves*.[14] In the words of Raymond Schwager, throughout the Bible "self-punishment and punishment at God's hand are not two distinct realities."[15]

This concept is clearly expressed in Paul's graphic description of "the wrath of God" that has been "revealed from heaven" in Romans 1.[16] God judged the sinners Paul has in view when "God gave them over" to "the sinful desires of their hearts," to their "shameful lusts," and to "a depraved mind,"[17] In this

10. See G. Boyd, *God at War: The Bible and Spiritual Conflict* (Downers Grove, IL: InterVarsity); G. Boyd, "Principalities and Powers" in *Dictionary of Scripture and Ethics, ed.* J. Green (Grand Rapids, MI: Baker Academic, 2012), 611–13.

11. John 12:32; 14:31:16:11; 2 Cor 4:4; Eph 2:2; 1 John 5:19.

12. Eph 2:1, 5.

13. For a full defense of this position, see G. Boyd, *Crucifixion of the Warrior God: Interpreting the Old Testament's Violent Portraits of God in Light of the Cross*, 2 vols (Minneapolis, MN: Fortress, 2017), 2:767–890.

14. E.g., Ps 7:14–16.

15. R. Schwager, *Must There Be Scapegoats: Violence and Redemption in the Bible*, trans. M. L. Assad (New York: Crossroad), 65. For a list of authors who defend this perspective, see Boyd, *Crucifixion of the Warrior God*, 2: 832, n.41.

16. Rom 1:18.

17. Rom 1:24, 26, 28.

light, it's significant that the only action ascribed to God when Jesus stood in our place as a sinner is that God "gave him up" and "delivered him over" to violent people who, operating under the influence of fallen powers, brought about the death consequences of the sin Jesus bore.[18] That is how Jesus experienced God's judgment on sin.

So long as we are deceived and in bondage to the powers and our fallen nature, we will suffer the destructive-consequences that are inherent in our sin. We are, as we saw, "by nature, objects of wrath." Jesus needed to enter into solidarity with our humanity, and then with our sin and curse, to free us from this deplorable state and to thereby reconcile us to God. For only the unsurpassable love of God that was manifested on Calvary was powerful enough to abolish the powers of darkness and to thereby free us to have our hearts compelled and our lives transformed by the love of God.[19] When I claim that, on the cross God bore God's own judgment on sin in order to accommodate us as sinners, *this* is what I mean.

Paul says that Jesus died for all so that "[they] might no longer live for themselves, but for the one who died for them."[20] And it is precisely because God is "not holding peoples' sin against them"—precisely because God is accommodating our sin—that God creates space for the Spirit to continue working in our fallen hearts to teach us and empower us to no longer "live for ourselves but instead to live for the one who died for [us]."

Moreover, as I've already mentioned several times, if the cross reveals what God is truly like, it reveals what God has always been like. The cross thus reveals that God has always been willing to accommodate sin and to suffer because of it. The theme is pervasive throughout God's story, as I've demonstrated

18. Rom 8:32; 4:25; cf. John 3:16.

19. 2 Cor 5:14–16. Reflecting the "rich variety" of "the wisdom of God" (Eph 3:10), there are a multitude of other things the cross accomplished as well. See J. B. Green, "The Kaleidoscopic View," in *The Nature of the Atonement: Four Views*, eds. J. Beilby and P. Eddy (Downers Grove, IL: InterVarsity Academic, 2006), 157–85. While I heartily embrace this diversity, I nevertheless advocate a *Christus Victor view of the atonement**, for I believe all the other things the cross accomplished are predicated on the defeat of the kingdom of darkness. See G. Boyd, "The Christus Victor View" in *Nature of the Atonement*, 23–49.

20. 2 Cor 5:15.

elsewhere.[21] For our present purposes, however, two illustrations must suffice.

* * *

God's original idea was for Israel to not have a human king, but instead to demonstrate to the nations what it looks like for a people to acknowledge the Lord God alone as their king, since this was God's original ideal for humans.[22] Unfortunately, there came a time when the Israelites couldn't any longer place their trust in an invisible king, so they demanded to have a human king. The people told Samuel the prophet: "We want a king over us. Then we will be like all the other nations, with a king to lead us and to go out before us and fight our battles."[23] After expressing grief over being rejected as king by the people, and after having Samuel warn the Israelites about the austere demands that a king will place on them, Yahweh reluctantly acquiesced.[24]

To appreciate the full significance of this, it's important to know that the king played a central role in the religions of the ANE, for ANE people never separated politics and religion. Among other things, everyone assumed that the king had a special relationship with his nation's chief deity and that the fate of their nation, especially on the battlefield, largely depended on whether or not the king continued to find favor with this deity.[25] When the Israelites insisted on acquiring a human king

21. See Boyd, *Crucifixion of the Warrior God*, vol.2, *passim*.

22. Note that in Gen 1:26–28, humans are instructed to exercise dominion over the earth and animal kingdom, but *not over one another*. Hierarchies of power in human society only appear after the fall.

23. 1 Sam 8:19–20, cf. v.5.

24. 1 Sam 8:6–18.

25. See J. Day, ed., *King and Messiah in Israel and the Ancient Near East: Proceedings of the Oxford Old Testament Seminar* (Sheffield: Sheffield Academic Press, 1998); J. Walton, *Ancient Near Eastern Thought and the Old Testament: Introducing the Conceptual World of the Hebrew Bible* (Grand Rapids: Baker Academic, 2006), 280–85; J. J. Niehaus, *Ancient Near Eastern Themes* (Grand Rapids: Kregel, 2008), 35–41; A. M. Rodriguez, "Ancient Near Eastern Parallels to the Bible and the Question of Revelation and Inspiration," *Journal of the Adventist Theological Society*, 12/1 (2001), 43–44. On kingship throughout the ANE, see H. Frankfort, *Kingship and the Gods: A Study of Ancient Near Eastern Religion as the Integration of Society and Nature* (Chicago: University of Chicago Press, 1946).

"like all the other nations," they were at the same time insisting that Yahweh relate to them through their king like all the other nations. This is just what it meant to have a human king in the ANE.

Interestingly enough, this is pretty much how Yahweh appears in the story of God once God decided to accommodate the Israelites sinful lack of trust by giving them a king. Hence, whenever kings were on good terms with Yahweh, things tended to go well. But whenever they weren't, things tended to go poorly, if not catastrophically. When David counted his soldiers, for example, thereby reflecting that he placed more trust in his military power than in Yahweh, a "destroying angel" was unleased and killed seventy-thousand people![26]

Agreeing to working with this king-centered framework was a major accommodation on God's part. It meant that, for a period of time in the story of God, Yahweh would appear quite a bit like all the other king-centered deities of the ANE. At the same time, God demonstrated God's unfathomable ability to bring good out of evil by taking the fallen institution of human kingship and weaving it into messianic hope that runs throughout the OT! This, I submit to you, is a very clear example of the noncoercive God influencing God's people in the direction of truth *as far as possible*, but then stooping to accommodate the fallible, fallen, and culturally conditioned minds and hearts of God's people *as much as necessary*.

For the same reason, this is a clear illustration of God honoring the say-so of God's people, despite the fact that they are using their say-so in rebellious ways. Moreover, it's also important to note that, in all of this, God was honoring the personhood of God's covenant partners to the point that God allowed their fallen need for a human king to condition how God henceforth appeared in the God-breathed story of God.

* * *

This is also a clear illustration of how God's breathing involves God *acting toward* God's people as well as God allowing the

26. 1 Chr 21:14.

fallible, fallen, and culturally conditioned minds and hearts of God's people to act *toward God* and to thereby condition what results from God's breathing. Rather than coercively lobotomizing God's people into believing the full truth about God—something God's people obviously weren't yet capable of doing on their own—God humbly stooped to meet the Israelites where they were at. Reflecting God's loving relational essence, God chose to continue to further God's purposes in the world by remaining in covenantal solidarity with his unfaithful covenant partners. All of this reflects God acting toward God's people.

Yet, to the degree that the depictions of Yahweh as a rather typical king-centered ANE deity fall short of who God truly is and of how God originally wanted to relate to humanity, we should understand these depictions to reflect God humbly allowing the fallible, fallen, and culturally conditioned state of God's people to *act toward God* and to thereby condition how God appears as a result of God's breathing.

Once they got a king, the Israelites thought of Yahweh as a rather typical king-centered deity, and since God had given them say-so, God wasn't going to coercively force them to think otherwise. So, though it grieved God to do it, God stooped to bear their rebellious and culturally conditioned conception of Yahweh as God breathed the story of God. And this, I contend, is precisely how this and every other fallible and fallen depiction of God in Scripture bears witness to the revelation of God on the cross, where God accommodated the sin of the world and thus took on the appearance of a guilty, God-forsaken criminal.

* * *

My second illustration of God's accommodating nature concerns the fact that we can discern a progress of revelation throughout the biblical narrative, as theologians throughout church history have attested. It's not a strictly linear development, but I will now argue that the very fact that there is a development at all presupposes that God's previous revelations accommodated some fallible, fallen, and cultural conditioned aspects of the hearts and minds of God's people.

Defenders of biblical inerrancy who also embrace the concept of progressive revelation try to argue that God's revelation gets clearer and clearer throughout the biblical narrative, but they insist that earlier revelations were nevertheless perfectly accurate, so far as they went. Hence, for example, the Chicago Statement on Biblical Inerrancy affirms that "revelation in the Holy Scriptures was progressive" while denying "that later revelation" ever contradicts earlier revelations.[27] In this view, in other words, progressive revelation happens by God *adding* more truth to previous true conceptions, but never by God *correcting* previous misconceptions.

To be frank, I strongly suspect that this is a case of defenders of inerrancy wanting to have their progressive revelation cake while eating their doctrine of inerrancy too. It simply doesn't work. To the degree that people don't have a clear conception of God, they by definition have a foggy conception of God. And the only way to give people a clearer and more accurate conception of God is to help them abandon their foggier and less accurate conceptions of God.

If you affirm progressive revelation—and most theologians do—then I see no way for you to avoid accepting that certain portraits of God in Scripture are accommodations that to one degree or another do not accurately reflect God's true will and nature. Defenders of inerrancy have always resisted this move, for if one assumes that inspiration entails inerrancy, then admitting that any portion of Scripture is erroneous is tantamount to denying the plenary inspiration of Scripture. But I trust it is by now clear why there is nothing inconsistent about affirming the plenary inspiration of Scripture while acknowledging its errors, so long as our conception of divine inspiration remains anchored in the cross.

* * *

I'd like to flesh out the nature of progressive revelation a bit further by considering biblical depictions of God's attitude toward animal sacrifices. As I mentioned in chapter 1, everybody in the ANE offered sacrifices to the gods. They believed they

27. "The Chicago Statement on Biblical Inerrancy: Articles of Affirmation and Denial," Article V, page 3, at https://tinyurl.com/y3x9y6jj; accessed May 28, 2019.

were appeasing the gods by feeding them food, and they believed the aroma of the burnt offerings pleased the gods and attracted them to this feast.

Thankfully, biblical authors never depict Yahweh devouring sacrifices—though one discerns a trace of this ancient conception in the several biblical references to sacrifices as Yahweh's "food."[28] This improvement upon what we find throughout the ANE reflects the influence of the Holy Spirit gradually weaning God's people off a deeply engrained, culturally conditioned, misconception.

It's also clear, however, that ancient Israelites were not ready to let go of the belief that Yahweh enjoyed the burning aroma of these sacrifices, as is evidenced by the repeated references to Yahweh enjoying their "pleasing aroma."[29] And since the Holy Spirit will not revoke people's say-so to make them have only true ideas about God, she graciously accommodated this misconception.

Now, the very fact that everybody in the ANE sacrificed animals (and, all too often, children) long before the Hebrews came along proves that this practice did not originate with Yahweh. In fact, Yahweh at one point told the Israelites they were to "no longer sacrifice their sacrifices to goat demons" but were instead to sacrifice animals to Yahweh alone.[30] This suggests that the Israelites had already adopted the ANE practice of sacrificing animals to goat demons from their ANE neighbors, so Yahweh apparently decided that, since the Israelites weren't ready to let go of this barbaric ritual, it was better to have them making sacrifices to God than to demons. In the words of the fourth century theologian, Gregory of Nazianzus, God "cut off the idol, but left the sacrifices."[31]

It thus seems that the Spirit decided to accommodate the ancient ritual of sacrificing animals as a means of increasing the Israelites' loyalty to God as well as to redefine the meaning of

28. Num 28:2; Lev 21:8.

29. E.g., Gen 8:2; Ex 29:18, 25; Lev 1:9, 13; 2:9; 4:31; Nu 15:3, 7.

30. Lev 17:7.

31. Gregory of Nazianzus, "Fifth Oration: On the Holy Spirit," in *Nicene and Post-Nicene Fathers*, series 2, vol 7, trans. P. Schaff, H. Wace (Grand Rapids: Eerdmans, 1978), 326.

these sacrifices. Among other things, God used these sacrifices to graphically illustrate the need for repentance and the death consequences of breaking covenant with God. God also used this practice to prepare the way for the time when God would offer Godself up as a sacrifice on behalf of the entire world.

The strongest confirmation of the accommodating nature of these sacrifices, however, is that later authors make it perfectly clear that Yahweh actually despised them! "You have neither desired nor taken pleasure in sacrifices and offerings and burnt offerings and sin offerings," the author of Hebrews states.[32] So too, in a passage that Jesus would later quote, Hosea says that Yahweh "desires mercy, and not sacrifice."[33] And in Isaiah we read,

> I have more than enough of burnt offerings, of rams and the fat of fattened animals; I have no pleasure in the blood of bulls and lambs and goats. (Isa 1:11)

And a few verses later Yahweh adds,

> Stop bringing meaningless offerings! They have become a burden to me; I am weary of bearing them. (Isa 1:13)

Later authors were clearly capable of receiving truths that earlier authors were not, and one of these truths was that Yahweh is actually not at all pleased with the aroma of burning animal carcasses. These later depictions don't merely add to earlier less complete depictions: they *correct* them.

* * *

This doesn't mean that the earlier mistaken depictions of Yahweh commanding animal sacrifices and enjoying their aroma are any less fully God-breathed than the later depictions. It simply means that in breathing these earlier depictions, the cruciform God had to stoop to accommodate the fallen and culturally conditioned views and practices of God's people at the time.

32. Heb 10:8.
33. Hos 6:6.

The depictions of Yahweh enjoying animal sacrifices, together with all the other sub-Christ-like portraits of God in Scripture, bear witness to the truth that "Jesus Christ is the same yesterday, today, and forever."[34] God has always been doing, if in penultimate ways, what God does in an ultimate way on the cross: stooping to bear the sin of God's people and to thereby take on an appearance that reflects the ugliness of that sin. More specifically, these portraits testify that God always been a noncoercive relational God who humbly enters into solidarity with God's covenant partners, including with their fallen and culturally conditioned views of God, despite the fact that doing so conditions-for-the-worse how God appears in the story of God.

* * *

In the above cited passage from Isaiah, the Spirit breaks through to reveal that God is "weary of bearing" these "meaningless offerings." A number of other passages also reflect the grief and pain Yahweh endured as God bore the sin of God's people. Isaiah even likens God's pain to the pain of a woman's labor pains![35]

To appreciate the depth of God's pain in accommodating animal sacrifices, it's important to know that throughout the Bible God demonstrates a profound love and concern for animals.[36] God even includes animals in certain covenants.[37] Yet, because God refuses to depersonalize people by coercing them into having only true beliefs, God had to be willing to suffer and let the Israelites go on believing that God demanded and enjoyed the butchery of animals, just as other ANE deities did.

And now consider this: If we have reason to conclude that the commands to slaughter animals as an act of worship were accommodations, how much more reason do we have to

34. Heb 13:8.

35. Isa 42:14.

36. S. H. Webb, *On God and Dogs: A Christian Theology of Compassion for Animals* (New York: Oxford University Press, 2008); S. Bulanda, *God's Creatures: A Biblical View of Animals* (Greeley, CO: Cladach Publishing, 2008).

37. Hos 2:18.

conclude that the depictions of God commanding the Israelites to annihilate entire human populations as an act of worship were divine accommodations? It's frankly hard for me to imagine a conception of God that is more contrary to the true heart of God, as revealed in Jesus's cross-centered life and ministry!

Hence, if God experienced something like labor pains bearing the sin of animal sacrifices, how much unimaginably greater must God's pain have been when God's people believed Yahweh wanted them to "utterly destroy" (*herēm*) indigenous populations throughout Canaan, and to do so as an act of worship?[38] Just as later prophets made it unmistakably clear that Yahweh never actually wanted animals killed, Jesus made it unmistakably clear that Yahweh never actually wanted people killed. Indeed, as we've seen, Jesus made the call to reflect the Father's character by loving enemies and refusing to engage in violence is the precondition for being considered a child of the Father.[39]

I submit that the progress of revelation that we see in Scripture, together with the closely related pervasive pattern of God bending God's ideals to accommodate sin, confirm what we've already learned about the relational way God breathes. As is true of the cross, God's breathing involves God both *acting toward* humans, as much as possible, and also God accommodating sin and allowing it to condition what is produced as a result of God's breathing, as much as necessary.

* * *

I submit that all of the problems of the Bible are simply reflections of God accommodating the fallen, fallible, and culturally conditioned nature of God's covenant partners. And this is precisely how these problems bear witness to the one who accommodated all that is broken and sinful in the world on the cross.

Yet, there is a fourth and final aspect of the revelation of God on the cross that not only demonstrates why the Bible's problems are not genuine problems; it clearly discloses why

38. On the concept of *herēm*, see Boyd, *Crucifixion of the Warrior God*, 1:293–97.
39. Matt 5:39–44.

these problems are actually God-inspired *assets* to the unfolding story of God. We'll explore this dimension of the cross in the following chapter.

14.

Cruciform Beauty

> People often say that "beauty is in the eye of the beholder," and I say that the most liberating thing about beauty is realizing that you are the beholder. This empowers us to find beauty in places where others have not dared to look.—Salma Hayek

> For he grew up before him like a young plant, and like a root out of dry ground; he had no form or majesty that we should look at him, nothing in his appearance that we should desire him. —Isaiah 53:2–3

I was sitting on an ugly grey and black speckled sofa in the basement coffee lounge of the U of M library. I had just taken a sip of the truly awful machine-brewed coffee that I'd been abusing my body with all day long. I was still wincing in disgust as I set my paper cup down and looked up at the clock. It was three minutes after 8:00 p.m. With the exception of a fifteen-minute vending-machine-supplied lunch break, a twenty-minute mind-clearing walk, and a half dozen or so trips to the coffee machine and (not coincidentally) to the bathroom, this is where I'd been seated since 8:00 a.m., when the library first opened.

I couldn't believe twelve hours had passed. I had originally planned on leaving the library around 12:45 to attend the first of two classes I had that afternoon. In fact, my time in the library that morning was supposed to be focused on reading assignments for these two classes. That plan got scrapped.

See, a guy named Frank had just introduced me to the writings of C. S. Lewis, and for the first time in nine dark months I was beginning to have a glimmer of hope that life might not be the absurd, painful, pointless joke that it seemed to be at this point in my life. Once I dove into *Mere Christianity*, which I had begun the night before, any concern I had about my upcoming classes completely vanished from my mind.

By midafternoon I had completed *Mere Christianity* and had moved on to a collection of Lewis's essays entitled *God in the Dock*, which I mentioned in chapter 2. I was nearing the end of an essay that was misleadingly entitled "Meditation in a Toolshed" at the moment I sipped my gross coffee, winced, and looked up at the clock.

I say this title was misleading because it sounded so boring to me that I considered skipping it. And it wasn't one of the essays Frank had flagged me to read, as I mentioned in chapter 3. But I'm so glad I didn't skip it, because this essay turned out to be anything but boring! In this essay, Lewis discusses the important difference between looking *at* something and looking *along* something. Maybe it was because I was still a bit of a newbie to reading philosophy, or maybe it was because after twelve hours of nearly nonstop reading my brain was turning to mush, but for whatever reason, I was having a frustratingly hard time grasping this distinction, or at least grasping why it was so important.

As I returned my cup to the coffee table next to the ugly sofa, I was suddenly startled by a loud and surprisingly deep growl of frustration. It seemed to have spontaneously erupted out of the mouth of a female student with long red hair who had been studying rather intensively on a sofa adjacent to mine for the last hour or so. Clearly startled by how loud her grunt sounded in this otherwise quite library lounge, this student giggled nervously as she cupped her hand over her mouth in surprise. She stared at me for a moment with an embarrassed-though-adorable look on her face, which was now almost as red as her hair.

"Yes, you really *did* just do *that!*" I said with a chuckle. She and several other students sitting on a nearby sofa giggled. "I just don't get this shit!" she said as she held up a textbook on modal logic. "I know exactly how you feel," I said as I held up my copy of *God in the Dock*. And *that* was the moment the proverbial coin dropped in the slot. I suddenly realized I had gone from looking *at* a frustrated red-haired student to looking *along with* a frustrated red-haired female student.

As his boring title indicates, Lewis's meditation begins in a toolshed that he had visited earlier in the day. The toolshed was pitch black inside except for one beam of sunlight that crept through a cranny at top of the door. As Lewis starred at this beam of light, he could see nothing else in the shed except dust particles that were illuminated by the light. "Then I moved," he says, "so that the beams fell on my eyes." And he continues:

> Instantly the whole previous picture vanished. I saw no toolshed, and (above all) no beam. Instead I saw, framed in the irregular cranny at the top of the door, green leaves moving on the branches of a tree outside and beyond that, 90 odd million miles away, the sun.

From this, Lewis concludes: "Looking along the beam, and looking at the beam are very different experiences."[1]

It's the difference between two people sharing the euphoric experience of falling in love, on the one hand, and a scientist describing all the chemical reactions that cause this euphoria, on the other hand. "That," Lewis notes, "is the difference between looking *along* the sexual impulse and looking *at* it."[2] Similarly, Lewis writes,

> The mathematician sits thinking, and to him it seems that he is contemplating timeless and spaceless truths about quantity. But the cerebral physiologist, if he could look inside the mathematician's

1. C. S. Lewis, "Meditations in a Toolshed," in *God in the Dock: Essays on Theology and Ethics*, ed. W. Hooper (Grand Rapids: Eerdmans, 1970), 212.

2. "Meditation," 212.

> head, would find nothing timeless and spaceless there—only tiny movements of grey matter.[3]

So too, a neuroscientist could provide us with an exhaustive description of what was going on in this young lady's brain when she let out her frustrated involuntary groan. Yet, however comprehensive and detailed a description of looking *at* this red-haired student's brain might be, it could never capture the empathy and humor I experienced when I looked *along* this student.

The central point of Lewis's essay is that it makes a world of difference whether you're looking *at* something, or *along* something, and that both of these perspectives are valid and necessary. The experience of falling in love, in other words, has just as much claim to being real as the scientific perspective that analyzes the chemical reactions that cause that experience.

* * *

I can also remember the moment I first began to understand the difference between looking *at* the cross and looking *along* the cross, which brings me to the fourth and final aspect of the cross that is relevant to our understanding of the nature of God's breathing. It concerns the fact that we can only discern that the cross is the definitive revelation of God when we stop merely looking *at* the cross and begin to look at God, ourselves, and the world *along* the cross.

This distinction first occurred to me around fourteen years ago as I was wrestling with the question of how the depictions of God as a violent ANE warrior deity in the OT could be interpreted in a way that disclosed how they bore witness to the crucified Christ, as we've seen all Scripture is supposed to do. At one point in the course of my toiling, I found myself asking a question I'd never heard anyone ask before, though once I asked it, it seemed like the most obvious question in the world for a Christian to ask: *How does the cross become the definitive revelation of God for us?*

3. "Meditation," 212–13.

Prior to becoming a disciple of Jesus, Paul admitted that he had regarded Christ "from a human point of view."[4] Christ was for him just one of the untold number of people executed by the Romans. So, what did Paul see as a believer that he couldn't see as a nonbeliever?

I submit that the cross became the definitive revelation of God for Paul when he moved from looking *at* the crucified Christ to looking by faith *along* the crucified Christ, and so it is with all of us. Similar to what happened to Lewis in the toolshed, the cross becomes the definitive revelation of God for us when we, by faith, step into its light to see something that people can't see when they're merely looking *at* the cross—that is, merely looking "from a human point of view." And what we see by faith is that, in this crucified man, God was stooping an unsurpassable distance to enter into complete solidarity with our humanity, our sin, and our curse.

No amount of merely looking *at* the cross could have ever disclosed this truth. To experience it, we must, by faith, step into, and look along, the revelatory light of the cross.

* * *

This is why the cross is simultaneously revoltingly ugly and supremely beautiful to the believer. On its surface, the cross is revoltingly ugly, for it mirrors the ugliness of the sin and brokenness that Jesus is bearing. As Isaiah prophesied, there is nothing about the surface appearance of this suffering servant that would make us "desire him." Instead, he is "one from who others hide their faces."[5]

Yet, just as Lewis was able to see a sun "some 90 odd million miles away" once he stepped into the light beam and looked along its path, so too, once we by faith step into the revelatory light of the cross and look along its path, we are able to look through its revoltingly ugly, sin-mirroring surface to behold something supremely beautiful that we could never otherwise see. By faith, we see God displaying God's unfathomable love by

4. 2 Cor 5:16.
5. Isa 53:2–3.

stooping an unfathomable distance to become our sin and our curse. Whether they know it or not, this is how everyone who believes in the cross comes to hold this belief.

We might therefore say that the revelation of God on the cross is revolting ugly on its sin-mirroring surface, which everyone can see, but supremely beautiful in its depth, which faith alone can see.

Look *at* the cross, you see revolting sin-mirroring ugliness.

Look *along* the cross, and you discover unfathomable divine beauty.

* * *

Since the cross reveals what God has always been like, and since all Scripture is God-breathed for the ultimate purpose of pointing us to the cross, I submit that we should read Scripture with the awareness that God sometimes reveals God's beauty by stooping to bear the ugliness, foolishness, and fallibility of God's people. More specifically, we should read Scripture with the awareness that sometimes the surface meaning of a passage will not reflect what God is truly like; it will rather reflect the way God's fallen and culturally conditioned ancient people viewed God, for this is the sin that God is stooping to bear.

The revelatory content of such passages will not be disclosed by looking *at* them "from a human point of view," assessing their meaning by ordinary exegetical means. Rather, when we come upon any material that "is not worthy of God," as Origen put it, we must be prepared to exercise the same faith we use to discern the cross to be the definitive revelation of God. We must by faith look past the sin-mirroring surface of such material to behold God stooping to remain in solidarity with God's people, just as God did for the entire world on the cross.

In short, since all Scripture is God-breathed for the ultimate purpose of bearing witness to the crucified Christ, I submit that we must read Scripture knowing that we sometimes will only discern the revelatory content of a passage when we examine it while looking *along* the crucified Christ.

* * *

I would like to introduce a distinction at this point that I believe might help people get a better handle on what I'm talking about.

Jesus's cross-centered life and ministry allows us to make a distinction between *direct* and i*ndirect* revelations in Scripture. A direct revelation is when the Spirit managed to break through the fallible, fallen and culturally conditioned mind and heart of an author to accurately reveal what God is like. To the degree that this happens, depictions of God will point to the beauty of the humble, self-sacrificial character of God revealed on Calvary, for the crucified Christ is the one and only Word of God. And to this degree, we need no special faith to understand the revelatory content of a depiction of God.

Since the NT teaches that Jesus was without sin, the Spirit obviously confronted no resistance when inspiring Jesus to teach. All of Jesus's teachings, therefore, may be considered direct revelations. When Jesus teaches us that the Father loves like the sun shines and the rain falls and that we are to do the same, for example, we are free to believe it or not, but we don't need any special faith insight to understand *what it means*. Exegesis alone is sufficient to understand such revelations. And so it is whenever biblical authors depict God in Christ-like ways.

By contrast, an indirect revelation takes place whenever the Spirit, after influencing an author in the direction of truth as much as possible, humbly accommodates as much of this author's fallible, fallen, and culturally conditioned heart and mind as was necessary. To the degree that this is the case, the result of God's breathing will reflect the fallible, fallen, and culturally conditioned heart and mind of this author. And to this same degree, the surface meaning of a passage bears witness to the sin-mirroring ugliness of the cross.

We must interpret all such passages in light of the cross, exercising the same faith we use to see the cross as the definitive revelation of God. We must by faith look through the sin-mirroring surface meaning of such a passage to see the humble, cruciform God doing in a penultimate way what God does in an ultimate way on cross. God is stooping out of love to remain in solidarity with God's fallen, fallible, and cultural conditioned people.

Everything in Scripture that reflects the fallen, fallible, and cultural conditioning of its human authors bears witness to the cross in just this fashion. Viewed in light of the cross, every mistake, every contradiction, and every sub-Christ-like portrait of God becomes a sort of literary crucifix within the story of God that confirms that God has always been doing what God does in a supreme way on the cross.

The cross, in short, reveals what God has always been like, and what God has always been doing, at least since humanity was seduced into aligning ourselves with the fallen powers against God. God has always revealed God's beauty by being willing to humbly bear all that is ugly, and to therefore appear, on the surface, revoltingly ugly.

* * *

There is one further observation I'd like to make before I bring this book to a close in the next chapter. In part 1 of this book, we explored the various ways scholars have tried to hold fast to the inspiration of Scripture *despite* its mistakes, contradictions, and sub-Christ-like depictions of God. We can immediately see how misguided this is when we read Scripture while looking *along* the revelatory light of the crucified Christ.

As I noted in chapter 9, we wouldn't say that the cross is the definitive revelation of God *despite* the fact that it is, on the surface, revolting ugly. To the contrary, the cross is the perfect revelation of the unfathomably beautiful God precisely *because* the surface of the cross is revolting ugly. Were the surface appearance of the cross less ugly, its revelation of God would have been less beautiful. In other words, it is precisely because God was willing to go to the unsurpassable extreme of becoming supremely ugly as God bore our sin and our curse that the cross is the definitive revelation of the unsurpassably beautiful God.

In short, the cross is supremely beautiful precisely *because* it is at the same time supremely ugly.

When we read Scripture *along* the crucified Christ, we can say something similar about every one of its mistakes, contradictions, inaccuracies, and fallen, culturally conditioned sub-Christ-like depictions of God. Each and every one enhances the cross-centered authority of the Bible by bearing witness to a loving, relational God who is not afraid of entering into mutually influential relationships with humans, and who therefore honors the personhood and say-so of God's covenant partners, even when God breathes revelations of Godself through them.

Each and every one bears witness to a God who works by means of the power of the cross, which is the influential power of other-oriented love, rather than relying on coercive power to lobotomize God's people into having true thoughts about God. Each and every one bears witness to a God whose holiness or set-apartness isn't anything like the pseudo-holiness of the Pharisees whom Jesus confronted, a holiness that is concerned with appearances and that separates itself from sinners. To the contrary, every foolish, weak, and sinful aspect of the Bible bears witness to a God whose holiness leads God to enter into solidarity with God's foolish, weak, and sinful people, just as God does on the cross.

Consider this analogy: Jesus fellowshipped with prostitutes and tax collectors, and this ruined his reputation in the eyes of certain religious leaders. They were abiding by the old adage, "You know a person's character by the company that they keep." Because these leaders didn't trust Jesus's character, they were incapable or unwilling to look past surface appearances to see the magnificent love and grace that Jesus was displaying by embracing these people as friends. Jesus's scandalous friendships with the worst of sinners became, for these leaders, proof that Jesus was himself a drunkard, glutton, and among the worst of sinners.[6] But of course, Jesus wasn't any of these things. He simply loved and wanted to help all people, no exceptions.

In the same way, each and every one of Scripture's inspired imperfections reflect on the loving character of a God who is not afraid of entering into solidarity with people in the imperfect

6. Luke 5:29–30; 7:33–34; 15:1–2.

state in which God finds them. And God is willing to do this even if it tarnishes God's reputation among those who do not fully trust God's character as it is revealed on the cross and who therefore are unable or unwilling to look past surface appearances in God's story to understand the beautifully self-sacrificial thing that God is *actually* doing when God stoops to appear in sub-Christ-like ways.

* * *

What all this means is that we have an important choice to make when we come upon (say) the biblical portrait of God commanding Moses to have the Israelites engage in genocide. On the one hand, I find it impossible to imagine Jesus—who taught us to always show mercy, to love indiscriminately, and to abstain from violence—commanding his followers to show no mercy as they exterminate entire populations of people, including the women and children, as an act of devotion to him. If we fully trust that Jesus's cross-centered life and ministry reveals what God has always been like and what God has always been doing, then so far as I can see, we have no choice except to assess the surface meaning of this ghoulish depiction of God to be a reflection of the fallen and culturally conditioned way Moses and God's people in general sometimes conceived of God at this time.[7]

If we accept that all Scripture is God-breathed for the ultimate purpose of pointing us to the crucified Christ, however, we are not permitted to dismiss this depiction as nothing more than a reflection of the fallen and culturally conditioned beliefs of God's people at the time. Rather, knowing from the cross that God sometimes reveals Godself by stooping to enter into solidarity with God's fallen, fallible, and culturally conditioned people, we must consider this to be an *indirect* revelation of God. This means we must by faith look *along* the revelatory light of the cross to

7. The fact that Paul instructs us to reject any Gospel other than the cross-centered Gospel he preached, even if it be delivered by "an angel from heaven" (Gal 1:8). provides further reason for us to conclude that Moses was mistaken when he thought he heard Yahweh instruct him to have the Israelites mercilessly slaughter "anything that breathes" in certain regions of Canaan (Deut 20:16).

see through the sin-mirroring surface of this portrait to behold God stooping out of love to remain in solidarity with God's fallen and culturally conditioned people.

On the other hand, if we don't trust that Jesus's cross-centered life and ministry fully reveals what God is like and instead suspect that God is actually capable of commanding people to mercilessly exterminate entire populations, then the depiction in Scripture of Yahweh commanding this will be taken at face value. In this case, in other words, we will consider it to be a *direct* revelation. We will thus assume that looking *at* this portrait suffices to disclose its revelatory content. We will thus feel no need to examine this depiction while looking *along* the crucified Christ to discern a deeper cruciform meaning.

Similar to certain religious leaders in Jesus's day, we will in this case find we are incapable of discerning the love and grace of what God is *actually* doing—stooping to remain in solidarity with God's people. And we will be incapable of discerning this precisely because we are trusting that what the ancient Israelites *thought* God was doing was what God was *actually* doing.

In sum, if we fully trust the humble, other-oriented, enemy-embracing, loving character of God as it is revealed on the cross, we will find this God revealed throughout the entire Bible, including all of its sub-Christ-like depictions of God as well as in all of its other imperfections. If we don't fully trust this character, however, then the Bible's sub-Christ-like portraits of God as well as its other imperfections become mere problems that we must futilely try to minimize or explain away, lest they tarnish God's character.

As the NT itself presents the matter, everything hangs on whether or not we are willing to fully trust the character of God revealed on the cross. What we find when we open God's story will say at least as much about the faith we *bring to* God's story as it does about what is actually *contained in* this story.

Anchor your faith in the crucified Christ, and you'll discover him everywhere in Scripture, including in its errors, mistakes, inaccuracies, and morally offensive material, including its sub-Christ-like depictions of God.

Anchor your faith in anyone or anything else and you'll find in Scripture lots of problems, including problematic depictions of God that contradict the revelation of God in the crucified Christ.

15.

Back to the Conundrum

> Rethinking gives you permission to use your thoughts to change your mind. Take what is and spin it around to give you a new review and fresh perspective. —Susan Young

> The scripture cannot be annulled. —John 10:35

I thought it only fitting to bring this book to a close by returning one last time to the conundrum that got me wrestling with the Bible's problems in the first place. You will recall from chapter 3 that, after recovering my faith in Christ, I found myself caught between the Charybdis of Jesus's authoritative endorsement of the OT and the Skyla of all the problems I knew were in it. The Cruciform Model of Inspiration is my proposed way out of this challenging conundrum.

This model of inspiration stipulates that, when understood in light of the cross, the Bible's problems are no more problematic to it being considered the God-breathed story of God than the sin and curse that Jesus bore on the cross are problematic to it being considered the God-breathed definitive revelation of God. All the foolish and weak aspects of the Bible reflect the wisdom and power of God for the very same reason the foolish and weak-appearing cross reflects the wisdom and power of God.

I've argued that this model of biblical inspiration enables us to agree with Jesus's view that all Scripture is God-breathed without needing to be embarrassed or troubled by the human foolishness and weakness that pervades Scripture. Indeed, when viewed through the lens of the cross, all the errors, contradictions, inaccuracies, and morally offensive material in Scripture point to the God who is definitively revealed on the cross. They bear witness that God has always been willing to stoop as low as necessary to enter into solidarity with sinners and to bear their sin, thereby, taking on an appearance that reflects the ugliness of their sin.

But is the Cruciform Model of Inspiration *really* compatible with Jesus's view of Scripture? Yes, it enables us to agree with his conviction that all Scripture is God-breathed. But is it consistent with *everything* Jesus taught about Scripture, according to the Gospels? In this chapter I will examine the two teachings of Jesus concerning Scripture that are most commonly appealed to by defenders of inerrancy and that pose the biggest potential scriptural objections to my proposed model of inspiration.

* * *

The first passage I'd like to look at—and the passage that will occupy the bulk of this chapter—is Matthew 5:17–18. Here Jesus says,

> Do not think that I have come to abolish the law or the prophets; I have come not to abolish but to fulfill. For truly I tell you, until heaven and earth pass away, not one letter, not one stroke of a letter, will pass from the law until all is accomplished.

According to the Cruciform Model of Inspiration, all OT laws that are inconsistent with the revelation of God in the crucified Christ—such as laws requiring the execution of children, gay people, fornicators, priests who enter the tabernacle with disheveled hair—reflect the Israelites' fallen and culturally conditioned beliefs about what God willed rather than what God actually willed. But if Jesus had to fulfill every letter and even every stroke of a letter of the law, then, one could argue, every stroke of a letter must reflect what God *actually* willed. Were any OT laws divine accommodations, one could argue,

Jesus would hardly have felt the need to fulfill them, let alone fulfill every last stroke of a letter.

Does this teaching of Jesus undermine the Cruciform Model of Inspiration? To no one's surprise, I will argue that it does not. In fact, I will argue that, when this passage is understood in light of the way Jesus actually treated Scripture throughout his ministry, this passage actually supports this model of inspiration.

* * *

To begin, Jesus's claim that he had come not "to abolish the law and prophets but to fulfill (*plerosai*), them" can be understood in two different ways. This statement could be taken to mean that Jesus had come to *meticulously obey* the law and the prophets, or it could be taken to mean that Jesus would *fulfill the true intention of the law and prophets and bring them to completion.* I am in agreement with those scholars who argue that the second interpretation is the only really viable one.[1]

The first option is problematic on a number of accounts. Among other things, *plerosai* doesn't normally refer to meticulous obedience. It rather usually has the connotation of completing something. Moreover, while it would make sense for Jesus to claim he would meticulously obey the law, it would be unnatural for him to claim to meticulously obey the law *and the prophets*, since prophets weren't primarily associated with giving commandments. Not only this, but as a matter of fact, Jesus *didn't* meticulously obey the law, as I will show in a moment. By contrast, we find a good deal of support for the second understanding of *fulfill* in the teachings of Jesus and in several NT authors.

1. E.g., K. Ward, *What the Bible Really Teaches: A Challenge to Fundamentalists* (London: SPCK, 2004), 23; C. L. Bloomberg, *Matthew* (Nashville: Broadman Press, 1992),106; D. Flood, *Disarming Scripture: Cherry-Picking Liberals, Violence-loving Conservatives, and Why We All Need To Learn to Read the Bible Like Jesus Did* (San Francisco: Metanoia Books, 2014), 14. For a fuller discussion of the meaning of this passage and of Jesus's treatment of Scripture, see G. Boyd, *Crucifixion of the Warrior God: Interpreting the OT's Violent Portraits of God in Light of the Cross,* 2 vols. (Minneapolis: Fortress, 2017) 1:67–91.

When Jesus was asked about "which commandment in the law is the greatest," he replied,

> You shall love the Lord your God with all your heart, and with all your soul, and with all your mind. This is the greatest and first command. And a second is like it: "You shall love your neighbor as yourself."

And then Jesus added, "On these two commandments hang all the law and the prophets."[2]

At the time of Jesus, the word translated as "hang" (*krememai*) was a technical term for laws that were derivable from other, more fundamental, laws. Jesus was thus claiming that everything written in the law and prophets is derivable from the commandments to love God and neighbor. Which means that the ultimate intention of everything found in the law and prophets was to help people love God and neighbor.

The significance of this remarkable teaching is reflected in the fact that it was adopted by the early church. It's reflected in Paul when he writes to the Romans:

> Owe no one anything, except to love one another; for the one who loves another has fulfilled the law. The commandments, "You shall not commit adultery; You shall not murder; You shall not steal; You shall not covet"; and any other commandment, are summed up in this word, "Love your neighbor as yourself." Love does no wrong to a neighbor; therefore, love is the fulfilling of the law.[3]

Love fulfills the whole law, which is most likely why James refers to the command to love your neighbor as "the royal law" and why Paul elsewhere refers to it as "the law of Christ."[4]

In this light, it seems natural to understand Jesus's claim to have come to "fulfill the law and prophets" to mean he had come to live out the true intention of the law and prophets, which ultimately is to help people love God and neighbor. After all, Jesus was the perfect embodiment of love, and, as Paul said, "love is the fulfilling of the law." Jesus also fulfilled the law

2. Matt 22:36–40. Jesus is here bringing together Deut 6:5 and Lev 19:18.
3. Rom 13:8–10; cf. Gal 5:14.
4. Jas 2:8; Gal 6:2.

and prophets by being the culminating revelation that is "their destined end," as one scholar put it.[5]

As we saw in chapter 8, everything in the OT points forward to, and is fulfilled in, Jesus's cross-centered life and ministry. The revelation of God in Christ thus completes and transcends the law, which is why Paul could proclaim that "Christ is the end of the law."[6] And if Jesus was indeed claiming that he had come to fulfill the law and prophets by living out their true intention and by bringing them to completion, there clearly is no incompatibility between this teaching and the Cruciform Model of Inspiration.

* * *

We also have to wonder why Jesus felt the need to publicly deny that he had come "to abolish the law." First century Palestinian Jews expected religious teachers to uphold and interpret the law. So, who among Jesus's audience could have ever suspected that Jesus would want to abolish it?[7]

The answer is, *the Pharisees*. And the Pharisees thought this because, as I noted in the previous chapter, to them Jesus's *looked like a law breaker*. Not only did Jesus scandalously befriend prostitutes, tax collectors, and other sinners who the Pharisees judged most harshly, but he repudiated and broke a number of OT laws. For example, Jesus once said,

> You have heard it told to the men of old, "You shall not swear falsely, but shall perform for the Lord what you have sworn." But I say to do, Do not swear at all, either by heaven, for it is the throne of God, or by the earth, for it is his footstool. [8]

Interestingly enough, Israelites were instructed in the OT to swear oaths in the name of God.[9] Hence, when Jesus prohibited

5. W. D. Davis, *The Setting of the Sermon on the Mount* (Cambridge, UK: Cambridge University Press, 1963), 100.

6. Rom 10:4.

7. For much of the following argument I am indebted to Derek Flood, *Disarming Scripture*.

8. Matt 5:33–34.

9. Deut 6:13.

all oath swearing, he was by implication instructing them to disobey an OT commandment. In fact, Jesus immediately added that the temptation to *obey* this OT command, or to say anything more than a simple yes or no, "comes from the evil one."[10] Whether or not Jesus had this in mind when he gave this teaching, it clearly implies that the desire to obey the command to swear by God's name is a temptation from the devil.

Jesus then moved on to replace the three eye-for-an-eye type commands in the OT with his instruction to "not resist one who is evil," followed by his teaching to "turn the other cheek" when struck, to give more of yourself than what is asked, and to love and bless our enemies.[11] It does not seem that Jesus was very concerned with preserving every stroke of a letter of these three OT commands, any more than he was with preserving every stroke of a letter of the OT command to swear by God's name. In this light, it's not surprising the Pharisees accused Jesus of abolishing the law.

Not only this, but the fact that Jesus replaced these commands with more loving commands lends further support to the view that Jesus intended to fulfill the law not by meticulously obeying it, but by living out its true intention, which we have seen is all about love. And what we are seeing here is that, sometimes to fulfill the spirit of the law, one must be willing to break the letter of the law.[12]

* * *

While Jesus considers the entire OT to be divinely inspired, he nevertheless pushes back on aspects of the OT more frequently than I think most people realize. For example, the OT law makes a clear and emphatic distinction between the kinds of foods that are kosher and the kinds of food that render you "unclean" and are therefore forbidden. But Jesus taught that "nothing going into a man from the outside can defile him." In this way, Jesus made "all food clean."[13]

10. Matt 5:37.
11. Matt 5:38–45.
12. See 2 Cor 3:6.
13. Mark 7:19.

Similarly, the law stipulated that any woman who bled was unclean and that anyone she touched became unclean, which meant they were not to touch anyone else until they had ceremonially purified themselves.[14] Yet, when a woman with a bleeding disorder touched Jesus, hoping to be healed, Jesus didn't rebuke her as a lawbreaker. He instead praised her courageous faith![15] Moreover, Jesus didn't immediately withdraw from the crowd to avoid contaminating others or to purify himself, as the law required.

The law also stipulated that people could not engage in any work on the Sabbath. In fact, as we mentioned in chapter 1, a person could be stoned to death for simply picking up sticks or lighting a candle in their home on that day of the week.[16] But Jesus displayed a more relaxed attitude toward the Sabbath, even defending his disciples when they violated a Sabbath law that prohibited harvesting food.[17]

So too, when Jesus was confronted with a woman who was guilty of adultery, he subverted the OT laws that demanded she be stoned.[18] In fact, Jesus refuted this woman's accusers by saying: "Let anyone among you who is without sin be the first to throw a stone at her."[19] Jesus's response presupposes that the only people who would be justified carrying out laws commanding capital punishment are those who are "without sin." Since everyone sins, Jesus's teaching functionally subverts all the capital offenses in the OT.

In this light, it seems that Jesus had a more nuanced understanding of the inspiration of the OT than his contemporaries. He certainly believed everything in the OT

14. Lev 15:25–27.

15. Luke 8:43–48.

16. Num 15:30; Exod 35:2–3.

17. Mark 2:23–28.

18. John 8:1–11. On adultery as a capital offense, see Deuteronomy 22:22 and Leviticus 20:10. I should mention that the earliest manuscripts of John lack this story, and when it shows up in the manuscript tradition of the NT, it does so in no less than five different places. Nevertheless, a number of considerations have led some scholars to conclude that this story goes back to the historical Jesus. See C. Keith, "Recent and Previous Research on the *Pericope Adulterae* (John 7:53–8:11)," *Currents in Biblical Research* 6, no. 3 (2008): 377–404.

19. John 8:7.

was God-breathed, but this clearly didn't mean that he believed everything in the OT reflected God's true will.

* * *

Jesus pushed back on other aspects of the OT as well. For example, James and John were angry when certain towns in Samaria rejected their Gospel message, so they asked Jesus if they could call down fire from the sky to incinerate them.[20] In the case of these two "sons of thunder," Jesus's teachings about loving and blessings enemies had clearly fallen on deaf ears. At the same time, James and John had a clear precedent for their request in the OT, for Elijah had called down fire from heaven to incinerate a hundred men in this very region.[21]

Although Elijah is generally depicted as a hero of the faith in Scripture, and although the fire that fell from the sky was clearly supernatural, Jesus *rebuked* his disciples for wanting to follow Elijah's example. Some early manuscripts add that Jesus suggested that James and John were of a "different spirit" than he. If this reading is accepted, as I'm inclined to think it should be, Jesus was suggesting that Elijah's destructive miracle had a demonic quality to it.[22]

* * *

Jesus pushed back on aspects of the OT not only by what he said, but also by what he *didn't* say.[23] Perhaps the best illustration of this took place when Jesus preached his inaugural sermon in his hometown synagogue. He read the first few verses of Isaiah 61, which declare:

20. Luke 9:54.

21. 2 Kgs 1:10–12.

22. As to how an OT saint could bring about a demonic destructive miracle, and for confirmations in the narrative itself (2 Kgs 1:1–10) that Elijah was acting contrary to God's will when he used his prophetic power in this murderous fashion, *see* G. Boyd, *Crucifixion of the Warrior God*, 2: 1195–1248. On the issue of whether or not Jesus's comment about a "different spirit" is in the original text, see Boyd, *Crucifixion*, 1:79n153.

23. This is a frequent strategy of Paul's as well. See D. Flood, *Disarming Scripture*, 7–70.

> The Spirit of the Lord God is upon me, because the Lord has anointed me to bring good tidings to the afflicted; he has sent me to bind up the brokenhearted, to proclaim liberty to the captives, and the opening of the prison to those who are bound; to proclaim the year of the Lord's favor, and the day of vengeance of our God.[24]

Except Jesus omitted the second half of the last line of his Isaiah quote! And what made this omission particularly significant is that waiting for God's vengeance to fall on Israel's enemies was a central feature of his audience's messianic hope. For his hometown audience, Jesus had just omitted the punch line of this passage! Jesus then had the audacity to add, "Today this scripture has been fulfilled in your hearing?" How could this passage possibly be "fulfilled," his audience would have been thinking, if its punch line was missing? And besides, they wondered, "Is this not Joseph's son?"[25] They were basically asking, "Who does this son of a local carpenter think it is?"

The audience's response to Jesus is opaque. Most translations, including the NRSV, have something like, "And all spoke well of him, and wondered at the gracious words that proceeded out of his mouth."[26] However, if the response of Jesus's audience was positive, as this translation indicates, why did Jesus reply by saying, "no prophet is acceptable in his own country?"[27] This response suggests that Jesus understood his audience's response to be entirely negative.

The best explanation for this, in my opinion, is that the word *martyreo*, translated above as "spoke well," can also mean to bear witness *against* a person. Moreover, the word *enthaumazon*, translated above as "wondered," can also mean "shocked." It seems to me that Jesus's response makes a lot more sense if his audience was *shocked* at his gracious words and spoke out *against* him rather than if his audience was *amazed* at his grace and spoke *well* of him.

But even if shock and anger weren't his audience's first

24. Isa 61:1–2, cf. Luke 4:18–19.
25. Luke 4:22.
26. Luke 4:22.
27. Luke 4:23–24.

response to him, it certainly was their second. For Jesus went on to tell them two stories from the OT that involved a prophet of Israel passing by fellow Jews who were in need in order to minister to gentiles.[28] Jesus was thus suggesting that, not only is God not going to smite the gentile enemies of Israel, but many who assume they are insiders on the things of God (Jews) are going to find themselves on the outside, while many whom everyone assumes are outsiders (gentiles) are going to be made insiders.

When his audience heard this, they were so "filled with wrath" that they plotted to push Jesus off a cliff![29] Jesus's hometown crowd didn't want good news that blessed their enemies while failing to guarantee their own insider status.

In light of all this, it's again not hard to understand why the Pharisees might have thought Jesus intended to abolish the law and prophets. The truth is that Jesus had come to fulfill them by living out their true intention and by providing the definitive revelation of God that brings them to completion. But if your eye is only on the letter of the law rather than on its spirit, and if "the love of God is not in your heart," as Jesus told the Pharisees, then the only thing you will see in Jesus is someone who sometimes breaks and replaces OT laws while keeping unsavory company.[30]

In any event, a viable model of biblical inspiration must be consistent not only with Jesus's teachings on Scripture but also with the way Jesus actually interacted with Scripture. It must therefore be able to affirm the full inspiration of Scripture while also making sense of the various ways Jesus pushed back on aspects of the OT. I submit that this is precisely what the Cruciform Model of Inspiration allows us to do.

* * *

The second teaching of Jesus on Scripture that defenders of inerrancy frequently appeal to and that may seem to stand in tension with the Cruciform Model of Inspiration was given

28. Luke 4:26–27.
29. Luke 4:28–29.
30. John 5:43.

in response to the Pharisees allegation that Jesus was guilty of blasphemy for claiming to be the Son of God. Jesus replied,

> Is it not written in your law, "I said, you are gods"? If he called them gods to whom the word of God came (and scripture cannot be broken), do you say of him whom the Father consecrated and sent into the world, "You are blaspheming," because I said, "I am the Son of God?"[31]

Jesus was basically arguing that the Pharisees were mistaken for thinking he was a blasphemer when he claimed to be the Son of God since their own law (which included the Psalms) referred to people as gods.[32] What interests us, however, is that Jesus said Scripture "cannot be broken" (NRSV, NASB, ESV, ASV) "set aside" (NIV), "discredited" (GWT), "altered" (NLT), "annulled" (NRSA), or "abolished" (CEB).

One could argue this teaching conflicts with the Cruciform Model of Inspiration inasmuch as this model claims that, to the degree that any passage conflicts with the revelation of God in the crucified Christ, its surface meaning at least can and should be broken, set aside, or annulled. Yet, in this passage, Jesus claims that God's word cannot be "broken," "set aside," or "annulled."

The first thing I'd say in response to this argument is that the very fact that Jesus repudiated and broke certain OT laws and taught people to do the same, as we've just seen, means that, when Jesus claimed that Scripture cannot be "broken," he couldn't have meant that every passage of Scripture must be *adhered to*, *believed*, and *obeyed*.

Secondly, Jesus's teaching in this passage is predicated on the assumption—shared by his opponents—that Scripture cannot be broken *when it is interpreted rightly*. Here is where Jesus and his opponents parted ways. They had very different perspectives on how to rightly interpret Scripture. As the Gospels portray them,

31. John 10:35.

32. Actually, Psalms 82, which Jesus is here citing, refers to divine members of Yahweh's heavenly council as "gods" (Ps 82:1). Yet, Jesus applies the passage to humans. Whatever else might be said about this curious exegetical move, it would seem to entail that the dignity that permits divine beings to be considered gods is also present in humans.

the Jewish leaders who opposed Jesus focused on meticulously observing certain laws, like "tithing mint and dill and cumin." According to Jesus, however, these leaders "neglected the weightier matter of the law, justice and mercy and faith."[33] So too, his opponents tended to focus on external, visible, behavioral matters while Jesus instead focused on people's hearts and minds.[34] In Jesus's words, his opponents were guilty of "straining out a gnat and swallowing a camel."[35]

Most importantly, while Jesus acknowledged that the Pharisees "search the scriptures" because they "think that in them [they would] have eternal life," Jesus added that it is these very Scriptures that "bear witness to me," the one who alone is the "life" of Scripture. Yet, for all their studying, the Pharisees refused to believe in Jesus, which is why their studying was devoid of life.[36] Moreover, Jesus explained to these Pharisees exactly *why* their reading of Scripture didn't lead to believing in him when he told them, "you have not the love of God within you."[37]

There is a good deal of legitimate debate about the origin and nature of the exegetical practices of Jesus and the authors of the NT, but I believe Jesus's teaching in this passage reflects the most fundamental driving exegetical principle of both. Jesus and his disciples were convinced that Scripture will only accomplish what it was inspired to accomplish when it is interpreted with the love of God in our hearts and with the conviction that all of it bears witness to Jesus, who is the perfect embodiment of the love of God.

Augustine hit the nail on the head when he introduced his famous exegetical "rule of love," which stipulates that "scripture enjoins nothing but love."[38] If we ever arrive at an interpretation of a passage of Scripture that is not consistent with love, argues Augustine, we have not yet arrived at the correct interpretation

33. Matt 23:23.
34. Matt 23:6–7, 25–28. Cf. Matt 5:21–30; Mark 7:14–23.
35. Matt 23:24.
36. John 5:39–40.
37. John 5:42.
38. Augustine, *On Christian Teaching*, trans. R. P. H. Green (Oxford: Oxford University Press, 1997), 76.

of that passage.[39] In fact, this rule has been advocated in one form or another throughout church history, though I will register my opinion that it has rarely been applied to Scripture *consistently*.

In any event, when Scripture is consistently interpreted in this love-centered, Jesus-centered, and ultimately cross-centered way, it cannot fail to accomplish what it was inspired to accomplish, which, as we've seen, is to lead us to the one who is the very life of Scripture, Jesus Christ. It is in this sense that I believe Scripture "cannot be broken." In this sense, Scripture is infallible, as I argued in chapter 8. When it is interpreted through the lens of the cross, which is John's very definition of love, it will never fail us.

At the same time, interpreting Scripture in this cross-centered way will require us, as it did Jesus as well as Paul, to sometimes break or repudiate the letter of Scripture in order to capture its spirit. In the terminology of the Cruciform Model of Inspiration, reading the Bible in this cross-centered way will sometimes require us to look with the eyes of faith *along* the crucified Christ to see through the sin-mirroring surface of a passage in order to behold the beauty of a God who has always been willing to stoop as low as necessary and enter into solidarity with people in the fallen and fallible condition God finds them.

Which, not coincidentally, is precisely what God does on the cross.

* * *

In light of what we've covered in this chapter, I don't believe either of the teachings of Jesus on Scripture that we've examined in this chapter are inconsistent with the Cruciform Model of Inspiration. To the contrary, I contend that this model of inspiration is more consistent with everything Jesus taught about the OT and with the way Jesus and the authors of the NT actually treated the OT than is the inerrancy model. Yet, the Cruciform Model has the additional advantage of not only freeing us from any worry about the Bible's alleged problems but also of disclosing how these problems bear witness to the

39. Augustine, *On Christian Teaching*, 27.

crucified Christ and are therefore divinely inspired assets to the authority of Scripture.

I, for one, consider that a significant advantage.

Postscript: Beautiful Scars

We probably all know the story. The other disciples informed Thomas that the tomb was empty and that they'd encountered Jesus resurrected from the dead. Thomas wasn't buying it: "Unless I see the nail marks in his hands and put my finger where the nails were and put my hand into his side," he insisted, "I will not believe."[1] He got his chance a week later.

The most surprising aspect of this exchange, in my opinion, is that Jesus's resurrected body retained the scars of his crucifixion. We of course know next to nothing about the nature of Jesus's resurrected body or of our future resurrected bodies, but I would have thought that, at the very least, our resurrected bodies would lack all the ugly scars we acquired on this side of eternity.

A serious accident when I was twelve required me to have an exploratory operation that left me with a thick, ugly scar extending down from my chest to my bellybutton. As a kid I was embarrassed by it, to the point that I never went without a shirt in public. While I've lost that embarrassment as an adult, I would still prefer a torso without a large unnatural zipper running down the front. So, if heaven is all it's cracked up to be, I would have thought my resurrected body would be free of my unsightly scar and that the same would hold true of everyone's resurrected body.

Yet Jesus, the firstborn from among the dead, retained his scars. And given that these scars were acquired from being crucified by Romans, they couldn't have been pretty. I used to

1. John 20:25.

suspect that perhaps Jesus supernaturally reproduced these scars just to fulfill Thomas' request. While this isn't impossible, I no longer think it the most likely explanation.

In Isaiah, Yahweh is depicted as a mother who could never forget the children she nursed, for their names were "engraved . . . on the palms of [her] hands."[2] While we usually consider scars to be unsightly, the scars in this depiction are beautiful, for they tell the story of God's faithful, motherly love. It now seems to me that Jesus's scars serve a similar purpose. I suspect Jesus retained those scars because they forever tell the story of his costly love for us, and this is a beautiful story that ought never stop being told. While Jesus's scars must have been ugly, considered by themselves, they contribute to the beauty of the resurrected Christ once we understand the story they tell.

Sometimes, the imperfections of a person or a thing can contribute to their beauty.

* * *

I once knew a woman who accidently broke a beautiful vase that happened to be a family heirloom into several pieces. Though she despaired that her cracked vase would never approximate the uncracked beauty of the original, she nevertheless sought out a professional who could restore as much of its former beauty as possible. Better a precious heirloom vase with scars than no heirloom vase at all.

Her search happened to lead her to a woman who specialized in Kintsugi, which in Japanese means "golden joinery." Instead of repairing broken pottery by trying to hide the cracks (and being embarrassed to the extent they still remain visible), practitioners of Kintsugi use a bright gold lacquer that *highlights* these cracks. For while Westerners typically want restored pottery to look as close to the original as possible, practitioners of Kintsugi believe it is neither possible nor desirable to try to replicate the original. By transforming cracks into bright gold lines, Kintsugi artists rather aim at *improving upon* the original.

Yet, this Kintsugi artist told my acquaintance that she'd only

2. Isa 49:16.

be able to appreciate how her post-broken vase was an improvement over her pre-broken vase if she was willing to stop clinging to the idea of getting as much of her pre-broken vase back as possible and to instead begin to look for all the ways the highlighted cracks in her vase give it a new and deeper kind of beauty.

It understandably took this lady a little time to get used to her vase's new look, but she told me that before long she absolutely fell in love with the Kintsugi version of her vase. Not only could she see how these bright cracks contributed to its overall beauty, but she could also see how they made her vase more precious by beautifully embodying a piece of its unique history, and of her own unique history. In this way, these golden cracks transformed this lady's heirloom into an altogether unique masterpiece. No longer was her vase *a type of* beautiful vase. Her vase was now *this particular* uniquely beautiful vase.

Moreover, this lady came to see how her masterpiece told a particular unique story of hope rising out of hopelessness and beauty rising out of brokenness. In fact, she shared that these cracks greatly increased her personal connection to her vase because they now had something in common: a story of brokenness and restoration. In fact, for her, those beautiful cracks became a symbol of her own brokenness and of her need to always trust that God is working in her to "turn her ashes into beauty," as one of her favorite worship songs put it.[3] But to appreciate this, my friend had to be willing to let go of her previous dream of getting as much of her pre-broken vase back as possible.

* * *

I was in a similar position once I lost my faith during my first semester at the U of M. What got shattered was not a vase, but my view of the Bible. Like most young evangelicals, I had been taught that the Bible was a perfect, errorless, heirloom of the Christian faith. Then, like a precious vase shattering on the

3. K. Scott, "At the Foot of the Cross (Ashes to Beauty)."

ground, I discovered it wasn't. It had problems, or, if you will, *scars.*

Like the scars on Jesus's resurrected body, these were scars I had assumed that God's inspired story wasn't supposed to have. For seven years I sought out specialists who I thought might help restore my Bible to as much of my former perfect ideal as possible by removing, minimizing, or quarantining these scars, but the ugly scars remained, and they were embarrassing. But then, with the help of Karl Barth, I finally let go of my former idea of what I thought the Bible was supposed to be and began to acquire a Kintsugi-like way of understanding it. I came to see that, when viewed *along* the crucified Christ, those scars stopped being ugly and stopped being an embarrassment. It's as though the light of the cross transformed these scars the way the gold lacquer used by Kintsugi artists transformed the cracks in my friend's vase.

I came to see that, when viewed in light of the cross, those scars contribute to the beauty and spiritual authority of Scripture by telling a story. And as is true of the beautiful scars on Jesus's resurrected body, the story these scars tell is a mini-version of the beautiful story told by the cross.

These scars tell the story of an adventurous relational God who is not afraid to give say-so to others in hopes of partnering with them to carry out God's will "on earth as it is in heaven."

These marks of human fallibility tell the story of an all-wise God who is able to accomplish God's objectives—including God's objective of bequeathing to the church a divinely inspired record of God's story—by using fallible, fallen and culturally conditioned people just as they are.

The fault-lines in Scripture tell the story of a faithful God who has always been willing to stoop as low as necessary to accommodate the weakness and sin of God's people in order to remain in covenantal solidarity with them and to continue to further God's purposes through them.

These apparent blemishes in Scripture tell the story of an avant-garde God who regularly defies our commonsense assumptions, a God who reveals God's omnipotent power and unlimited wisdom by appearing weak and foolish, and a God who points people to the cross by means of an often weak and foolish-appearing Bible.

And as was true of my friend with the Kintsugi-reworked vase, I have found that this cross-centered, Kintsugi-like understanding of the Bible's once-troublesome scars has significantly deepened my personal bond with Scripture. I can see my own brokenness reflected in all the characters that show up in God's story (save Jesus), and I can readily identify with the sin and imperfections of the authors God used to breath God's story. If God was able to use those fallen and fallible people to bring about the story that would serve as the foundation for the community of God's people and the means by which people would come into a relationship with Christ, then there surely is hope for the rest of us fallen and fallible people. If God was able to transform the unsightly brokenness and scars of biblical authors into something that displays God's glory, then I can trust that God can do the same with my own brokenness and my own scars as well as with the brokenness and scars of everyone else. Indeed, C. S. Lewis notes that, precisely because God left these imperfections in the Bible, we are able to "re-live, while we read the whole Jewish experience of God's gradual and graded self-revelation, to feel the very contentions between the Word and the human material through which it works."[4]

In other words, in the story that all the Bible's scars tell, we can find the story that all of our own scars tell, if we will but surrender them to God. And it is always a version of the same story the cross tells. It's the story of a Kintsugi God who is able to build God-glorying masterpieces using human weakness and sin as building material.

In sum, when viewed in light of the cross, there is no more need to be embarrassed by the Bible's scars then there is to be embarrassed by the scars on Jesus's resurrected body—if only we can set aside our old assumptions about what a God-inspired story is *supposed to* look like and instead boldly embrace the cross-centered story of God that we *actually have*.

It may not be the Bible many of us were taught to expect. But

4. C. S. Lewis, "Reflections on Psalms," in L. W. Dorsett, ed., *The Essential C. S. Lewis* (New York: Simon & Schuster, 1988), 404.

it is precisely the kind of Bible I believe we should expect from a God who, in the person of Jesus Christ, acquired deep scars that he now wears like a crown.

Glossary

Ancient Near East (ANE): The area that roughly corresponds to the Middle East today. All ANE nations, including the ancient Israelites, shared a number of basic beliefs and practices, such as the assumption that God/gods delight in animal sacrifices.

Arminian/Arminianism: Reflecting the thought of Jacob Arminius (1560–1609 CE). In contrast to Calvin, who taught that God unconditionally chose, before the creation of the world, who will and will not be saved, Arminius taught that God's choice of who will and will not be saved was based on God's foreknowledge of who will and will not freely choose to believe. Today, however, the label "Arminian" is often applied to any Christian who denies the Calvinistic doctrine of unconditional election and who affirms that humans have libertarian (viz. not compatiblisic) free will, regardless of whether or not they believe God foreknew who would and would not freely choose to believe before the creation of the world.

Bibliolatry: When the Bible is revered to the point that it stops being a book we look *through* to see Jesus and begins to function as an idol we look *at*, as though it was a source of revelation distinct from Jesus.

Cappadocian fathers: Refers to three theologians who ministered in Cappadocia, which is in modern day Turkey. These are

Basil "the Great" (330–379 CE), who was bishop of Caesarea, Gregory of Nyssa (ca. 335–ca. 395 CE), who was Basil's younger brother, and Gregory of Nazianzus (329–389 CE), who became Patriarch of Constantinople. They are best known for their reflections on the Trinity and are credited with originating the doctrine of the perichoresis of the three divine Persons.

Christus Victor (view of the atonement): The understanding that the primary way Jesus's death on the cross saves us and redeems creation is by defeating the kingdom of darkness. It was the dominant understanding of the atonement for the first thousand years of church history.

Classical theologians: Theologians who espouse "the classical view of God," which has been the dominant view of God among Christian theologians since the fifth century. This view stipulates (among other things) that God is "*actus purus*" (pure actuality, devoid of potentiality), "immutable" (never changes in any respect), "impassible" (never suffers), "atemporal" (experiences no before or after), and altogether "simple" (is not comprised of different parts).

Compatiblistic Freedom: The belief that morally responsible human free will is compatible with God determining all that comes to pass (or, outside of Christian circles, with all things being determined by some other means). In this view, humans can be said to be free if there is nothing preventing them from getting what they want, even though what they want has been predetermined.

Critical OT [or NT] scholars/scholarship: Scholars who rely on historical-critical tools to interpret Scripture and who, at least in theory, operate outside of any faith commitment. Most critical scholars hold that it lies outside the bounds of academic scholarship to ever appeal to supernatural causes to explain history, though not all would conclude that this means that it's never rational to believe in supernatural occurrences.

Crucicentric: Centered on the cross. The conviction permeating this work is that a consistent Christocentric approach to Scripture requires us to adopt a crucicentric approach to Scripture.

Cruciform Model of Inspiration: An understanding of how God breathes that is anchored in the crucified Christ, understood as the definitive and paradigmatic revelation of God. In this model of inspiration, God breathes Scripture both by acting toward humans and by allowing humans to act toward God and to thereby condition what results from God's breathing, just as God does on the cross. Moreover, according to this model of inspiration, God sometimes breathes revelations of God's beauty by stooping to accommodate the sin of God's people, thereby taking on a semblance that reflects the ugliness of that sin, just as God does on the cross.

Documentary Hypothesis: The view that the first five books of the Bible are comprised of at least four originally independent sources, J (Jahwist), E (Elohist) P (Priestly), and D (Deuteronomist). Scholars argue that these sources can be distinguish from one another by their distinctive styles, vocabulary (including differing names for God), concerns, disagreements from one another on certain factual matters, and different theological perspectives. First developed in the 19th century, it has become the dominant model among OT scholars, though it has been significantly modified and supplemented by an assortment of scholars over time.

Epistemic: Having to do with what we know and how we know it.

Historical-Critical Approach to Scripture: A method of studying Scripture that treats it no differently than it would treat any other ancient collection of writings. Among other things, historical-critical scholars try to discern the various possible sources that may have been combined in the construction of a biblical narrative. And they try to determine the historical veracity of these sources, though they often vary widely in their determinations.

Historic Orthodox Christianity: Historically, Christians have generally considered the founding Ecumenical Creeds, and especially the Apostles Creed and the Nicene Creed, to define the parameters of orthodoxy. Any group that deviates significantly from any of the core convictions expressed in these creeds is, by definition, outside the parameters of historic orthodox Christianity.

Naturalistic: Philosophically, "naturalistic" refers to anything pertaining to the "naturalistic worldview," which holds that the physical world alone is real. In this view, it is assumed that all reports of miraculous occurrences are either fraudulent or legendary.

Passion narratives: The Gospel narratives of Jesus's suffering, from his arrest to the crucifixion.

Paradigmatic: Sets the example, model, or paradigm by which other things are understood. Since all the treasures of God's wisdom are found in the crucified Christ (1 Cor 1:18, 24; Col 2:2–32). I contend that the cross should be considered to be the paradigmatic example of God breathing. Hence, it is the example by which God's breathing of Scripture should be understood.

Pentateuch: The first five books of the Bible, traditionally ascribed to Moses.

Perichoresis: Mutual Indwelling. The Cappadocian fathers used this concept to describe the relationship of the three Persons of the Trinity.

Plenary Inspiration of Scripture: The church's traditional belief that the whole Bible is fully inspired. Among other things, this belief prohibits Christians from simply dismissing biblical passages because of the moral, historical, scientific, or theological problems they pose. Rather, each and every passage of Scripture must be considered God-breathed for the ultimate purpose of pointing people to the crucified Christ, notwithstanding their possible moral, historical, scientific, or theological problems.

Pre-critical: The perspective of people reading Scripture (or anything else) prior to the Enlightenment, when scholars, and later the general population, first began becoming aware that the world of the biblical text may not always conform to the world of what we can determine actually happened. Many scholars today contend that, to read Scripture as the inspired story of God, we must assume a pre-critical mindset.

Progressive evangelicals: A very diverse group of people who continue to embrace many of the distinctives of evangelicalism, including the importance of having a personal relationship with Jesus, but who tend to emphasize the social justice aspect of the Gospel while embracing at least aspects of the historical-critical approach to Scripture.

Redacted/ Redaction Criticism: According to critical Bible scholars, much of the Bible was compiled by weaving together previous oral and/or written sources that scribes altered, or "redacted," to form a single narrative. By paying attention to how redactors altered their material, scholars are able to approximate what the source material of a narrative was like prior to its being redacted into its canonical form.

Synergism: The belief that God influences, but does not coerce, human wills. Hence, whenever God's will is accomplished through people, it's because *both* God and these people willed it to happen. The antithesis of synergism is monergism, which holds that God's will alone determines what comes to pass.

Synoptic Gospels: Refers to the Gospels of Matthew, Mark, and Luke, because they share so much content over and against the Gospel of John.

Textual critics: Scholars who meticulously comb through ancient manuscripts and fragments of manuscripts to determine when a scribal alteration might have entered the textual tradition. In this way they work to get us back as close to the original reading as possible.

Theological determinism: The belief that God determines all that comes to past.

Theological Interpretation of Scripture: A theologically diverse group of (mostly) Bible scholars and theologians. Yet, they share the conviction that there is a great difference between reading the Bible in a historical-critical manner and reading the Bible as the inspired story of God. Among other things, to read the Bible as the inspired story of God requires us to assume a pre-critical posture as we read and/or hear it.

Author Index

Achtemeier, P., 46
Augustine, 89, 163–64

Barth, Karl, xxii, 49, 53–81, 85–87, 90, 94–95, 97, 112, 125, 170
Bauckham, R., 65, 91
Beegle, D. M., 44
Beilby, J., 22, 70, 128, 130
Berkouwer, G. C., 45
Boyd, Gregory, xi, xvii–xviii, 7, 21–22, 34, 42, 49, 56, 64, 69, 88, 94, 115, 120–21, 129–31, 138, 154, 159
Bray, G., 119
Bromiley, G. W., 61, 69, 79, 90
Bruce, F. F., 22
Bulanda, S., 137
Bultmann, R., 22

Camus, Albert, 16
Carsen, D. A., xvii
Chalke, S., 128

Davies, P. R., 10
Davis, W. D., 156
Day, J., 131
Dockery, David, 50
Dolezal, J., 119
Dörner, I. A., 119
Doyle, Sir Arthur Conan, 37

Earl, Douglas S., 67
Eddy, Paul, 21–22, 34, 42, 56, 70, 128, 130
Enns, P., xv, 67

Fee, G., xxii
Fiddes, P., 119
Flood, D., xv, 154, 156, 159
Frankfort, H., 131
Frei, H., 61
Fuller, D., 46

Gavrilyuk, P., 118
Gish, D., xii
Gorman, M., 88, 92
Green, J. B., 92, 129–30

Green, Michael, 37
Gregory of Nazianzus, 135, 174

Hallman, J., 119
Hardin, M., 128
Hartshorne, C., 119
Hayek, Salma, 140
Heron, Alasdair, 37
Hick, John, 37
Hitchens, Christopher, 72
Hull, B., 61

Jami, Cassi, 116
Jersak, B., 128

Kafka, Francis, 16
Kähler, M., 92
Kahnaman, D., 23
Kane, R., 120
Keener, C., 23, 91
Keith, C., 158
Koch, K., 45
Kraft, C., 46
Kreeft, P., 120

Lehmann, H. T., 94
Lemche, N. P., 10
Lencioni, Patrick, 106
Lewis, C. S., 15, 17–25, 54, 141–44, 171
Luther, Martin, 93–94

Michaels, J. R., 45
Migliore, Daniel, 54
Moltmann, Jürgen, xviii, 85, 93, 119
Moody, Andrew, 91
Morris, H., xii

Niehaus, J. J., 131
Nietzsche, Fredrick, 16

O'Connor, T., 120
O'Donovan, J. L., 89
O'Malley, Martin, 44
Origen, xv, 47, 49, 67, 145

Packer, J. I., 45
Pascal, B., 49, 93
Paul, xvi, 12, 33–35, 58, 64, 67–68, 88, 92–93, 101, 105, 111–12, 115, 117–18, 120, 123, 129–30, 144, 149, 155–56, 159, 164
Pelikan, J., 94
Pinnock, C., 45
Price, R. M., xxii, 44

Ramm, B., 45
Rodriguez, A. M., 131
Rogers, J., 44–45
Russell, F. H., 89

Sartre, Jean Paul, 3, 16
Schwager, Raymond, 129
Schweitzer, A., 33
Seibert, E., xv
Stuart, D., xxii

Tomlin, Graham, 93-94
Torrance, T. F., xviii, 61
Treier, D. J., 61

Walton, J., 131
Ward, K., 154
Warfield, Benjamin B., 30
Webb, S. H., 137
Weinandy, T. G., 119

Whitcomb, J., xii
Witherington, Ben, 31
Wood, A. S., 93
Wright, N. T., 33, 64, 92, 128

Young, Susan,152

Zia, M. J., xxii

Topic Index

Ancient Near East (ANE), 6–8, 56, 126, 131–35, 137, 143, 173
animal sacrifices, 8, 135–38, 173
  ascribing violence to god a form of praise, 135–36
  parallels with Bible, 8
  and warrior gods, 8
archeology, xvi, 6, 10, 98
atheism, xiv, 17–18
atonement, 80, 128, 130, 174
  Christus Victor view of, 130, 174
  includes whole creation (cosmos), 24
  penal substitution view, 128
Augustine, 89, 163–64
  definition of love, 89, 164
  "rule of love, " 163

Barth, Karl, xxii, 49, 53–72, 74–81, 85–87, 90, 94–95, 97, 112, 125, 170
  atonement, 80
  deep literalism and the Bible, 61–62
  entering world of the Bible, 61, 66
  fallibility of Scripture, 55, 57, 60, 68–70, 76, 86, 112
  fideism of, 74–75, 79–80
  game-changer, 62, 70
  God breathes through sinful authors, 95
  God's condescension, 57, 68, 97, 125
  God's sovereignty and free will, 57, 69–70
  historish verses *geschichte*, 62, 66
  incarnation analogy of inspiration, 81, 86–87, 94
  inspiration as a dynamic event, 57, 59, 74, 76–81
  Jesus alone is Word, 76
  sinlessness of Jesus, 86
  verbal inspiration, 59, 77–78
  view of Bible, 60, 68, 77

view of cross, 80–81, 86–87, 95
Book of Mormon, 72–75, 79

Charybdis and Skyla, 28, 30–32, 36, 43, 152
classical view of God, 174
church, xi–xiii, xvi–xvii, xx, 3–4, 26, 34–36, 43, 47, 58, 61, 66–67, 80, 86–89, 106–7, 117–19, 122, 133, 155, 164, 170, 174, 176
Bible as rudder of, 4, 26
and inherited political power, 87
and models of inspiration, 107, 161–62
violent tradition of, 89
See also under Augustine; Scripture
Code of Hammurabi, 8, 12
creation, 5–6, 24, 42, 88, 113–14, 122, 125
cross/crucified Christ/ crucifixion:
all scripture points/bears witness to, 63–64, 66, 87, 91–92, 149
analogy of biblical inspiration, 86–87, 95
ascribing unsurpassable worth to humans, 90
as centerpiece of good news, 94
as definitive revelation of God, 80, 87–88, 107, 109, 112, 143–47, 152
as epicenter of Scripture, 87, 92
as essence of gospel, 65
foolishness (weakness, sin, problems) of Bible points to, 90, 153
God going to furthest extreme, 24
God suffers own judgment on, 128, 130
hidden treasures point to, xvii
“hour” Father glorified, 91
is/reveals the power of God, 105, 117–19, 145, 152
is/reveals the wisdom of God, 93, 97, 130
looking *at* versus looking *along*, 141–43, 150
as key to unlocking secrets of Christian theology, 85, 93–94
needing to fully trust, 149–50
offense of, 86
paradigm of God acting and being acted upon, 113–14
paradigm of God’s breathing, 114, 120, 176
paradigm of God stooping to accommodate sin, 89, 104, 127, 137, 144–45, 175
permeating all Scripture, xxiii, 174–75
revealing God becoming God’s antithesis, 24, 90
revealing God has always

accommodated sin, 112, 127, 133, 135, 138
revealing God in solidarity with our weakness, foolishness, 95, 104, 113, 128, 130, 133, 137, 144–45, 147–50, 153, 164
as revoltingly ugly and supremely beautiful, 144
should anchor all thinking about God, xv, 94, 108, 112, 150–51
as through-line of Jesus's ministry, xviii, 87, 91
as very definition of love (1 John 3:16), 89
Cruciform Model of Inspiration, 152–56, 161–64, 175

disciples, xvii, 11, 32–35, 40, 49, 64, 75, 88, 91, 103–4, 158–59, 163, 167
Documentary Hypothesis, 5, 175

Elijah, 127, 159
Elisha, 125–27
Emergent Church, xvii
Enuma Elish, 6
evangelicalism/ evangelicals, xiv–xx, xxii, 6, 17, 22, 26, 37–38, 41, 44–45, 53, 59, 67, 107, 112, 169, 177
assume perfect God must breath a perfect book, 38, 67
and inerrancy, 37–38, 41–43, 134
and qualified inerrancy, 44
evolution, xii–xiv

fallen powers /powers of darkness/ powers, 88, 110, 127, 129–30, 147,
defeated on cross, 88, 130
helped orchestrate crucifixion, 110, 129–30
humans in bondage to, 127, 129
faith, 42, 55–57, 59–62, 66, 68, 73–77, 86, 109, 127, 144–46, 149–50, 152, 158–59, 163–64, 169, 174
acting *as though*, 27
and aviophobia, 27
going beyond, but not against, reason, 76
as gift of Holy Spirit, 68
and God stooping in problems in Bible, 144–45
and God stooping on the cross, 145–46
free will, 57, 69, 7, 120–22, 173–74
and divine sovereign, 55–59, 68–70, 78, 80–81
irrevocable, 121
libertarian verses compatibilistic, 69–70, 173–74
our say-so, 115, 119–24, 132–33, 135, 170
synergism, 69, 177

genocide, 149
God:
  adventurous (risk-taking), 121, 170
  ascribing unsurpassable worth to humans, 90
  assailing common sense assumptions, 103
  beyond gender, xix
  breathing relationally, 105, 108
  choosing to love enemies, 138
  cruciform character, 104, 108, 122
  delivering Jesus over, 109
  and destructive consequences of sin, 129–30
  endowing agents with free will, 121
  entering mutually influential relationships, 120, 148
  grieving, 70, 131, 133, 137
  judging sin, 127
  human longings pointing toward, 20
  humility of, 121
  immutability and impassibility of, 118–19
  importance of mental picture of, 63
  as love, 89
  and love for animals, 137
  and love for creation, 24
  as nonviolent, xv–xvi, 135–36
  and pain of bearing/accommodating sin, 136–38
  poured out on cross, 113
  power as influential love, 118, 120, 122, 148
  power as lure of beauty, 118
  power as manifestation of love, 130
  power as willingness to suffer, 119
  respecting personhood of others, 119–21, 132
  revealing beauty by appearing ugly, 144
  as self-sacrificial, 90, 118, 146
  sovereignty of, 57, 69–70
  stooping to accommodate sin of the world, 89, 104, 127, 137, 144–45, 175
  suffering own judgment, 128
  taking on appearance of ANE deities, 8
  violent/morally offensive depictions of, xv, 4, 6, 58
  working by means of influence, not coercion, 35, 110
  working with partners/coworkers, 115, 123–24
  wrath of, 128–30, 161
  See also Holy Spirit; Trinity/triune God
gospel (good news):
  cross as essence of, 92

as greatest possible love story, 24–27
historical veracity of, 22–23
as true north of human heart, 25
Gospels, 21–24, 26, 30–32, 34, 42, 48, 92, 153, 162, 177
as centered on cross, 149
contradictions between, 31–32
differences between the Synoptics and John, 34
as extended passion narratives, 92
historical veracity of, 22–23
read as ancient literary documents, 21

historical-critical approach/ scholars:
and assumption of naturalism, 42, 176
and bias against miracles, 23
and differing conclusions, 48
open historical-critical approach, 42
and questions not answered by Jesus or NT authors, 66
redaction criticism/ redactors, 177
textual criticism/critics, 4, 177–78
historic orthodox faith/church, xvi–xviii, 3, 47, 176
and plenary inspiration, xvi, 48
plenary inspiration as bedrock assumption of, 47
history:
"actual history," 25, 45–46, 61–62, 66–67
and enlightenment, 177
Holy Spirit/Spirit, xxi, 13, 32, 34–35, 49, 59, 135
accommodating shortcomings, 124, 130
acting and allowing herself to be acted upon, 113–14
and feminine pronouns, xix–xx, 108
inspiring biblical authors, 34, 59
and religious experience, 75
revealing as much as possible, accommodating as much as necessary, 146
and search for an interpretation "worthy of God," xvii, 49
weaning God's people off misconceptions, 135
working by means of influence, not coercion, 35, 110

incarnation, xviii, 81, 86–87, 91–92, 94, 109
as fulfilled on cross, 86, 156
as reflecting God stooping, 89
inerrancy, 37–45, 45–46, 48, 111–12, 133–34, 153, 161, 164
God's perfection entails, 108

limited/qualified inerrancy, 44
one error refutes, 4, 47
and original autographs, 40
as safeguarding orthodoxy, 38
as vulnerable/dangerous to hold, 39
inspiration/God-breathed, xvi, 3, 5, 35, 58, 92, 136, 145, 149, 152–53, 176
as anchored in the cross, 94, 134, 175
as applies to entire Bible, 3, 36
dictation theory, 107–8, 110–11
and historical-critical scholarship/problems, xxiii, 174
human weakness and sin, 87, 171
as not perspicuous to all, 59, 76
of OT/NT, 30–35
problems as assets, xviii, xxi–xxii, 49, 139, 165
relational verses unilateral, 108
as seen by faith, 144–45
See also inerrancy; Scripture
Israelites, 6–8, 10, 76, 126, 131–38, 149–50, 153, 156, 173
ascribing violence to God a form of praise, 135–36
and animal sacrifices, 8, 135–38, 173
demand for a king, 131–33
fallen and cultural conditioned views of Yahweh, 127, 132–33, 136–37

Jesus/ Christ:
and call to love enemies, 12, 138, 157, 159
and call to nonviolence, 138, 149
as creating conundrum, 152
and criteria for being considered a child of the Father, 138
cry of forsakenness, 24
and focus on heart, not behavior, 163
fulfilling the law, 155–57
as fully God and fully human, 21, 58, 88, 95
and great mythology, 21
as impacted by others, 119
as the lens of Scripture, 66, 153, 164
as the "life" of Scripture, 163–64
myth become fact, 21
ordinary kings, 102
opposition by Pharisees, 163, 176
passion of, 92, 110
rebuking disciples, 159
reputation, 91, 148–49

as revelation of triune God, 55
same yesterday, today, and forever, 137
scars, 167–72
Scripture pointing to, 63–64, 66, 87, 91–92, 149
sinlessness of, 86
subverting capital punishment, 158
teachings as direct revelations, 146
as treasure of God's wisdom, xvii
unity of revelatory life, death, and resurrection, 77, 80
view of the OT, 5, 47
washing disciples' feet, 103–4
as Word of God, xxi, 55, 57–59, 63, 65, 146
as Word of God not tied to Bible, 59
See also atonement; cross; incarnation

Kintsugi, 168–71
Kintsugi God, 171

last supper, 98, 103
law, 8, 38, 64, 153–58, 161–63
love fulfills, 155
Jesus fulfills, 31, 155
Jesus repudiates aspects of, 156, 162, 164
letter and spirit of, 153, 157
referring to people as "gods," 162
Lewis, C. S., 15, 17–25, 54, 141–44, 171
case for believing in God, 18–22
case for believing Jesus is Lord, 17
love:
Augustine's definition of, 89, 164
and behavioral implications, 89
and cross, 89
as freely chosen, 122
as mutually influential, 120, 122, 124
as noun that God eternally is, 89
respecting say-so of others, 119
risk as price of freely chosen love, 90

Moses, 5–6, 29–30, 45, 64, 67, 149, 176
mishearing God, 149
as traditional author of Pentateuch, 5, 29, 45

Origen, xv, 47, 49, 67, 145
and hidden treasures, xvii
and inspiration of Bible's problems, xvii, 47, 49, 67
and passages "unworthy of God, " xvii, 145

Paul:
- "cross" and "gospel" interchangeable, 92
- cross as essence of gospel, 65
- and the cross/crucified Christ, 85, 93, 144
- God uses foolish and weak things, 97
- and heavenly vision, 118
- and knowing nothing save crucified Christ, 85, 93
- and looking *along* cross, 143

Pentateuch, 5, 29, 45, 67, 176
- and Jesus, 5, 45, 67
- *See also* documentary hypothesis

Pharisees, 29, 148, 156–57, 161–63
- diligently searching Scripture, 163
- focusing on behavior, 156–57, 163
- love of God not in heart, 161
- opposing Jesus, 163
- neglecting weightier matters of law, 163

progressive evangelicals, xv–xix, 177
- and historical-critical method, xv
- and plenary inspiration, xvii
- and violent depictions of God, xv–xvi

progressive revelation, 134

Quran, 75, 79

reciprocity, 69

relationships, xviii, xx, 8, 17, 20, 25, 63, 77, 80, 113, 122–23, 131, 148, 171, 176–77

resurrection, 31, 64, 87–88, 92
- and Christ's divinity, 57, 101, 119
- Jesus's scars, 167–72
- as part of cross event, 88, 91, 105
- as power of God at work in us, 87
- triumphalist interpretation, 87
- victory of cross, 87

revelation, xviii, 25, 55, 59, 65, 73, 76, 80, 85, 87–88, 90, 94–95, 97, 104–9, 112, 117, 120–21, 125, 133–34, 138, 143–47, 149–53, 156, 161–62, 173, 175
- direct and indirect, 146, 149

Scripture/Bible:
- all God-breathed/inspired, xvi, 3, 5, 35, 58, 92, 136, 145, 149, 152–53, 176
- ANE writings parallels, 6–8
- bearing witness to Jesus/ Christ crucified/ the cross, 63–64, 66, 87, 91–92, 149
- and bibliolatry, xxi, 173
- cannot be "broken, " 38, 162, 164

Christocentric entailing crucicentric, 174–75
and church needs, 4
and dismissing no text, 149, 176
entering world of biblical text, 61, 66
and error-free zone, 47, 112
fallibility/infallibility of, 55, 57, 60, 68–70, 76, 86, 112
historical veracity of, 22, 33, 46, 175
historish verses *geschichte*, 62, 66
inspired message verses cultural conditioned medium, 133, 147
interpretation and confirmation bias, 11
interpretation of, 154, 163, 178
interpret looking *along* crucified Christ, 145, 147, 150
literal interpretation of, xi, xiii, 33, 61–62
literary crucifixes, 147
and material "unworthy of God, " xvii
multiple authors/ perspectives, xxi
not secure epistemic foundation, 26, 175
plenary inspiration as bedrock assumption of church, 47
plenary inspiration includes problematic material, xvii
plenary inspiration of, xvi–xvii, xix, 5, 48, 53, 58, 111, 134, 176–77
pre-critical interpretation, 61, 66, 177
portions not anchored in history, 61
and problems, xiv, xxi, 25, 30–31, 38, 41, 151
reflecting foolishness and weakness of humanity, 90, 153
as rudder of ship, 4, 26
and scars, 171
as story of God, xxi, 7, 36, 70, 74–75, 77, 80, 95, 99–100, 114, 132, 137, 152, 178
surface meaning and sin, 145–46, 149, 162
trust, 47, 66, 69–70
uniqueness of, 6, 58, 80
as witness to the Word, xxi, 55, 58, 60–62, 68, 76

theological determinism, 69–70, 120, 123, 178
Trinity/ triune God, xx, 24, 55, 77, 90, 109, 113, 122, 174, 176
and cross, 90, 113
perichoresis, 113, 118, 174, 176

young-earth creationism, xii